MW00487517

demonstratives

definitive treatise
on visual persuasion

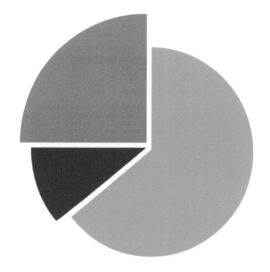

Daniel J. Bender   **R. Jason Fowler**   Pierre E. Kressmann

Cover design by Tahiti Spears/ABA Design.
Interior design by Betsy Kulak/ABA Design.

The materials contained herein represent the opinions of the authors and/or the editors, and should not be construed to be the views or opinions of the law firms or companies with whom such persons are in partnership with, associated with, or employed by, nor of the American Bar unless adopted pursuant to the bylaws of the Association.

Nothing contained in this book is to be considered as the rendering of legal advice for specific cases, and readers are responsible for obtaining such advice from their own legal counsel. This book is intended for educational and informational purposes only.

© 2017 American Bar Association. All rights reserved.

No part of this publication may be reproduced, stored in a retrieval system, or transmitted in any form or by any means, electronic, mechanical, photocopying, recording, or otherwise, without the prior written permission of the publisher. For permission contact the ABA Copyrights & Contracts Department, copyright@americanbar.org, or complete the online form at http://www.americanbar.org/utility/reprint.html.

Printed in the United States of America.

21 20 19 18 17   5 4 3 2 1

ISBN: 978-1-63425-951-4

e-ISBN: 978-1-63425-952-1

Discounts are available for books ordered in bulk. Special consideration is given to state bars, CLE programs, and other bar-related organizations. Inquire at Book Publishing, ABA Publishing, American Bar Association, 321 N. Clark Street, Chicago, Illinois 60654-7598.

www.shopABA.org

To my wife, Samantha, for her unwavering love, support, and dedication, and to the memory of my mother, Evelyn.

—DJB

To Robin, my mom, for always believing in me, and to Sarah, my wife, for agreeing to join me on this crazy adventure.

—RJF

To my wife, Rosa, for our decades of friendship, love, and life's ups and downs we have shared.

—PEK

Contents

Foreword

From Cave Paintings to Memes:
A Case for Visual Persuasion

From cave paintings to memes, pictures have served as a powerful form of communication. We live in an information age, where attention spans wane, social media reigns, and images bombard the eye. Yet the legal profession still relies mainly on the written and oral forms of communication rather than the visual. To ignore the visual form seems at best a missed opportunity and at worst an egregious mistake for lawyers, who seek to educate, enlighten, and persuade on behalf of clients on a daily basis. More often than not, the creation of a chart or graph to help make a point, or a timeline to explain the case, is a low priority, an afterthought, or something reserved for complex cases. However, visual aids can be a powerful tool in any case and should not be relegated to the bottom of the "to do" list.

Now more than ever, a book like this is needed. It's needed by the 99.9 percent of us who cannot write and orate brilliantly like Abraham Lincoln. It's needed by those of us who have clients who depend on us to win the day or limit the damage done. The authors get it. They've seen and lived through all manner of litigation and disputes, from high-stakes trials where a thoughtful and well-timed demonstrative exhibit can mean the difference between winning and losing, to a government agency meeting where a simple but effective chart can help lead to closure of an investigation. In this book they've given us everything from the theory behind advocacy design to the building blocks of visual illustration and style. The Inspiration Index alone, found at the back of this book and replete with outstanding examples, is a tremendous resource. I know that I will keep this book amply tabbed and close at hand.

Demonstratives require thought. They also take time and can be expensive. Like writing a good sentence, creating an effective demonstrative is not easy. When it's done right, however, it looks effortless. Demonstratives force you to think about your case in a different way, with clarity, visually, and in a way that a fact finder can easily absorb. Sometimes a simple chart is all that is needed. Other times, a complex timeline with call-outs and graphics is needed to sum up a case. As Professor Edward Tufte showed, evidence can be beautiful. Demonstratives can make the most complex set of facts more easily understood. As zealous advocates, we owe it to our clients to think creatively and help solve their problems with every tool at our disposal, especially the most powerful ones. This book will help all of us achieve that goal.

Mark Rosman
Wilson Sonsini Goodrich & Rosati
Washington, DC

Acknowledgments

We would like to thank Digital Evidence Group, LLC, for supporting us in the creation of this book. We would also like to thank Lawrence D. Rosenberg, co-chair of the American Bar Association Section of Litigation's Book Publishing Board, who guided this project from inception to publication.

The views expressed in this book are those of the individual authors, do not necessarily reflect the views of the American Bar Association, Covington & Burling LLP, or Digital Evidence Group, LLC, and should not be construed as legal advice.

About the Authors

Daniel J. Bender is an experienced litigator and, since 2007, has been a litigation consultant assisting trial teams from across the country developing strategies for and creating their demonstratives. Prior publications by Mr. Bender include:

Winning or Losing Your Case in the Blink of an Eye: An Exploration of the Intersection of Malcolm Gladwell's "Blink" and Litigation, LAW360 (Nov. 18, 2013).

Happy Holidays from the ITC, THE AM. LAW DAILY (Feb. 25, 2013).

My Odyssey: From Litigator to Litigation Consultant, AMERICAN BAR ASSOCIATION (Mar. 5, 2013).

The Art of Advocacy Design, AMERICAN BAR ASSOCIATION (Feb. 9, 2011).

Demonstratives on Direct, PRACTICING LAW INSTITUTE (Dec. 2009).

Alternative Dispute Resolution Manual: Implementing Commercial Mediation, IFC/WORLD BANK GROUP (Nov. 2006).

Limiting the Options, LEGAL TIMES (June 3, 2002).

New International Commercial Arbitration Evidence Rules Economize, Appeal to Common and Civil Lawyers, THE METROPOLITAN CORPORATE COUNSEL (Oct. 1999).

Case Commentary: In re Application to Quash Grand Jury Subpoena Duces Tecum Served on the Museum of Modern Art, N.Y.U. J. of Int'l L. & Pol. (Fall 1998).

An Alternative Approach to Settling Disputes over Stolen Art, N.Y.L.J. (Aug. 12, 1998).

Pierre E. Kressmann has decades of experience as a lead litigation graphic designer and trial consultant. He has worked in both in-house law firm and outside consultant environments, having developed concepts, graphics, and animations for hundreds of domestic and international cases in all areas of law for clients big and small. An accomplished graphic and fine artist, Mr. Kressmann received his degree in Painting and Illustration from East Carolina University.

R. Jason Fowler is a partner at Covington & Burling LLP, practicing in the firm's Litigation and Intellectual Property Groups. He was formerly an adjunct professor at Howard University School of Law, teaching Patent Practice & Procedure. In addition, he lectured for several years on patent law for the Patent Resources Group. Before private practice, Jason was a law clerk at the U.S. Court of Appeals for the Federal Circuit and the U.S. District Court for the Northern District of Georgia. Prior publications include:

Federal Circuit Patent Law, Patent Resources Group (2011-2012).

Lacks v. McKechnie *and the Quest for On-Sale Bar Certainty,* 38 Ga. L. Rev. 1369 (2004).

Introduction

Back in the "early days" of litigation practice, a lawyer would make an oral argument to a judge or ask questions of a witness who would answer orally. As years progressed, the lawyer may have enlarged a photograph or chart on an easel. But, with the advent of personal computers, the use of demonstratives has increasingly become a staple of the courtroom.

Lawyers now use a variety of computer software and hardware tools to display in the courtroom everything from exhibits, photographs, deposition video, and, of course, demonstratives.[1]

This book is an in-depth reference guide to the theory and practice of creating persuasive and effective demonstratives. The book dives deeply into the strategy of demonstratives. It explores issues such as when to use demonstratives, and perhaps more importantly, when *not* to use demonstratives, what stages of litigation could benefit from demonstratives, different uses for still and animated graphics, etc.

Within these pages you will find a common reference point for the verbal and visual language of demonstratives. Creating a definitive set of terms with accompanying illustrative images not only makes communication clearer and more efficient, but also sparks ideas for different approaches and looks for demonstratives. An "Inspiration Index" of visuals with examples is also included. This book is essential reading and a within-arm's-reach guide for every litigator.

---

1. Throughout this book, we use the term "demonstratives" as a convention for electronic and printed graphics that lawyers use in court, also commonly referred to as litigation graphics, trial graphics, trial demonstratives, etc.

Demonstratives Theory

Demonstratives are not just pictures, charts, events on a timeline, and so on. Demonstratives are key pieces of advocacy that, like a honed brief or oral argument, require strategy, experience, and execution. The effectiveness of demonstratives all starts with the thought process involved in creating them.

1

What Are Demonstratives?

Before an attorney or litigation support professional can embark upon the journey of making worthwhile demonstratives, they first need to know what demonstratives are. Not just the finished product of charts, pictures, graphs, animations, and so forth—but what demonstratives really are at their core. *Black's Law Dictionary* defines demonstratives as:

> Physical evidence that one can see and inspect (i.e., an explanatory aid, such as a chart, map, and some computer simulations) and that, while of probative value and usu. offered to clarify testimony, does not play a direct part in the incident in question.[1]

Just knowing *Black's* definition and that demonstratives are typically graphics or animation will **not** aid you in making effective and persuasive demonstratives. To do that, you first need to know what it is you are making, and why.

To have a true understanding of demonstratives, you first need to understand the difference between demonstratives, demonstrative exhibits, and demonstrative evidence. Many—if not most—attorneys use these terms interchangeably, but they are not the same things.

---

1. Black's Law Dictionary 675 (10th ed. 2014).

Although they are closely related, knowing the differences will allow you to use the terms with precision, which is helpful in dealing with your clients, other attorneys, and the court.

Demonstratives

Demonstratives:
advocacy graphics in legal proceedings

Figure 1—Demonstratives

What exactly are demonstratives? They are primarily advocacy graphics in the form of charts, graphs, illustrations, and animations.[2] Those advocacy graphics are generally used in a litigation setting as an aid to an attorney's argument or to support a fact or expert witness's testimony. Advocacy graphics are discussed at length in the next chapter, but what you need to know for the purposes of this discussion is that they are charts, graphs, illustrations, and animations that the attorney uses to persuade a judge or jury. They are not meant simply to provide facts, but are almost always meant to sway opinion.

Demonstratives must be truthful, credible, understandable, and memorable to be effective and persuasive. We discuss next how to apply the principles of advocacy design to create effective advocacy graphics.

In addition to trials and arbitrations, demonstratives can also be used effectively in hearings, client meetings, negotiations, mediations, expert reports, pleadings, etc. They can directly incorporate evidence, but doing so is not a requirement. Either way, demonstratives must be based on evidence and the law, not conjecture and speculation.

---

2. Physical models and the like can also be demonstratives but are not the subject of this book.

When demonstratives are used in evidentiary proceedings such as arbitrations and trials, they may be further subdivided into demonstrative exhibits and demonstrative evidence.

Demonstrative Exhibits

Figure 2—Demonstrative Exhibits

Demonstrative exhibits are demonstratives that a party in an evidentiary hearing has marked as exhibits during the proceeding. Sometimes judges or arbitrators require all demonstratives that a party intends to use be marked as exhibits, and sometimes there is no such requirement. Those demonstratives may have been created for use at the trial or may have been made earlier, such as those created for and used in an expert report or made for a deposition and marked as a deposition exhibit. There are also times when demonstratives may be used, but not marked as demonstrative exhibits. Two common examples are demonstratives used in support of opening and closing statements. It is possible that the same trial will have demonstratives that are not marked as exhibits as well as those that are (making them demonstrative exhibits). Given how highly variable this issue is depending on the particular tribunal (and even the particular jurist within the tribunal), it pays to find out how your judge or arbitrator deals with marking or not marking demonstratives as demonstrative exhibits by speaking with others who have practiced before them and with their law clerks.

Demonstrative Evidence

Figure 3—Demonstrative Evidence

Demonstrative evidence is the result of when a party moves the tribunal to admit into evidence a previously marked demonstrative exhibit. Given that demonstratives are created for litigation, they typically do not have probative value of their own, unlike, for example, a key underlying case document. As a result of their provenance, demonstrative exhibits are typically not entered into evidence. Although rare, there are times when demonstrative exhibits can be made into demonstrative evidence. When it does happen, it is quite advantageous for a case in court. Since demonstrative evidence is part of the evidence in the case, it has two key advantages over demonstrative exhibits.

"A look is better than a description."

—*Fowler v. Sergeant*, 1 Grant 355
(Penn. 1856)

First, demonstrative evidence, like all other evidence admitted in a case, can be reviewed by the jury in the jury room. This ability gives demonstrative evidence the potential for impact not only during the court proceedings, but also during jury deliberations.

Second, because demonstrative evidence is transmitted to the appellate court along with the rest of the evidence and transcripts as part of the record, if there is an appeal the demonstrative evidence has the potential to sway the appellate tribunal.

Summary

To sum up:

- Demonstratives are advocacy graphics used in legal proceedings.
- Demonstrative exhibits are demonstratives marked as exhibits in the case.
- Demonstrative evidence are demonstrative exhibits entered into evidence.

Now that we know the definition of demonstratives on an intellectual level, we can explore what they are in the physical realm. When you see demonstratives in the form of charts, graphs, illustrations, and animations, what is it that you are seeing? Typical demonstratives include:

- illustrations of underlying facts
- illustrations of analogies
- charts, graphs, and tables
- annotated maps
- document call-outs
- document comparisons
- timelines
- 3D illustrated still graphics
- 2D "flat" animations
- 3D "dynamic" animations

- narrated technology tutorials
- animations of physical, mechanical, chemical, or electrical processes
- animations creating or reenacting events

Demonstratives come in so many forms and are made in so many ways because of their almost limitless applications.

2

Advocacy Design: The Thought Behind the Images[1]

Demonstratives are advocacy graphics that attorneys use to inform and persuade a judge, jury, arbitrator, opposing counsel, etc. But an effective demonstrative involves more than just making a graphic and showing it in court. Advocacy design is the art of creating advocacy graphics. The person making the demonstratives is, as you may have guessed, the advocacy designer.

If you want effective and persuasive demonstratives, then the advocacy designer must be treated as a specialized adjunct member of the legal team for the limited purpose of visual presentation. Just giving orders to an advocacy designer without giving them the broader context may not produce results consistent with overall themes and will hamper the designer's ability to add value. The lawyers on the case will have lived with it for months or years. Advocacy designers are typically later

---

1. This portion of the book is an expanded adaptation of the article, *The Art of Advocacy Design*, by Daniel J. Bender, American Bar Association (Feb. 9, 2011).

additions to the team and can give a fresh perspective on approaches—but only when armed with context about the case. Before pen is put to paper or hand to computer, there should be meetings to discuss the case, themes, witnesses, issues, hurdles, etc. Because advocacy designers are often involved in more hearings and trials than the typical attorney, they can offer valuable insight into how a theme or fact may be interpreted by the finder of fact. Most litigators who hire professional advocacy designers do so because that is precisely the type of advice they are seeking. To be persuasive and have the desired impact on the target audience, the team should use the following analytical process.

Goal ➡ Strategy ➡ Visuals (G➡S➡V) Analysis

Advocacy design starts with **Goal ➡ Strategy ➡ Visuals (G➡S➡V) Analysis**. Oftentimes when it comes to creating demonstratives, an attorney will want to create a timeline showing, e.g., "what was being reported in the trade press prior to the purchase," "the email traffic before the contract was signed," "the prior art," or whatever other facts relate to a case. In this timeline example, the attorney is thinking of what facts he or she wants to show—i.e., the end product. But that approach is an end-run around the G➡S➡V Analysis and hampers the designer's ability to take what you want to show and turn it into an effective demonstrative.

Goal

G➡S➡V Analysis: **Goal**—Identifying a clear **Goal** is the "why" of the demonstrative. Everything that happens in the design process must be measured against whether or not it advances your goal. If showing something does not advance your goal, then it is merely a graphic for graphic's sake . . . and a waste of time, effort, and money. The goal can be based on a large case theme or on a particular legal or factual point. The key is to ensure that the graphics mesh with the overall presentation of facts and arguments in the case.

Let's turn back to the first timeline example—a timeline showing what was reported in the trade press prior to purchase. Why are those media reports important? What is the goal in juxtaposing them with the purchase date? The goal may be to show that the purchaser should have known what it was buying or to show that the seller's claims were in accord with the prevailing knowledge at the time. With the goal established, you are ready to start thinking about how to meet that goal.

Strategy

G➡S➡V Analysis: **Strategy**—**Strategy** is determining the best way to meet the established goal. Demonstratives strategy can take different forms depending on whom you are trying to influence and what you are trying to advocate. To develop an effective strategy, you need to answer questions such as: What information will you emphasize? Do you need to show documents? Would using visual analogies be effective and appropriate? What supporting data sets can you use? What is the best medium of the message? Do you need to use illustrations or animations? Answering these and other similar questions will help you reach your goal in an organized, methodical, and efficient manner.

Looking again at our timeline example, a timeline may be one way to show when trade press reports were being published compared to the time of the transaction. But there are other ways that may be more effective. Perhaps the timeline can be combined with a series of individual document call-outs showing the reporting. Maybe the call-outs can be stacked to show a virtual pile of evidence. Maybe that pile of documents does not even require a timeline, but perhaps just a list of the articles supportive of the party's position. An entirely different approach such as a graph showing frequency of the relevant news over time might make the point. Or maybe there could be a calendar with hyperlinks to key documents from specific days. These are just some ideas. Ultimately, the exact nature and type of data will help determine the best strategy to meet the goal.

Visuals

G→S→V Analysis: **Visuals**—If you know the goal of the demonstratives and have thought through the best strategy to reach the goal, the legal team is now ready to begin creating the **Visuals**. But this does not mean you are ready to fire up PowerPoint and start making graphics. It's time to consider design principles specific to demonstratives.

Design Principles

Implementation of three key design factors is required to help drive the persuasiveness of the visual: (i) Know the User, (ii) Lightning Speed Principle, and (iii) Differential Emphasis.

Know the User

Your demonstrative must be tailored for your audience. The necessary look, feel, and content of a demonstrative can vary greatly depending on the target audience's demographics and background. Is the presentation intended for a judge, jury, arbitrator, mediator, opposing counsel, or your client? What are the demographics of the target audience? These questions all help the advocacy designer understand for whom he or she is designing. They need to **Know the User**. When they do, they can custom tailor the demonstrative to the users of the information to make them as persuasive and impactful as possible.

Maybe you have a case in the U.S. District Court for the Northern District of California in San Francisco about the breach of a venture capital agreement. Given the higher-than-normal level of understanding about the tech world and its inner workings in the region, demonstratives may present a different level of detail than if the case were in a small rural district. But the inverse would be true if the case were a breach of contract matter about a farm equipment lease.

As an example, the following demonstrative with detailed patent drawings showing a chemical process likely would only be appropriate for someone with a relevant scientific background.

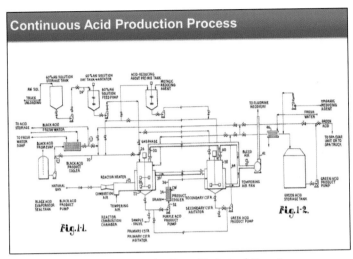

Figure 4—Know the User: Technical Drawing

The demonstrative above can be recreated as in the example below, making it more understandable to a lay audience. This demonstrative starts with the building blocks of the patent drawing, boils it down to the key processes, and makes it easier to comprehend. As previously explained, decision-makers are more likely to be persuaded by something that they understand.

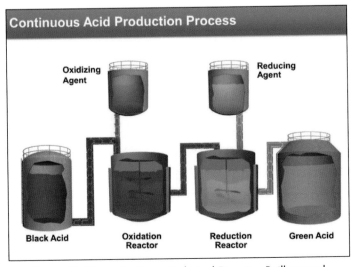

Figure 5—Know the User: Technical Drawing Reillustrated

Knowing the user and creating demonstratives with that user in mind helps ensure accessiblity of the information the attorney is conveying.

Lightning Speed Principle

The Lightning Speed Principle is the tricky step where the advocacy designer must make sure to communicate the point of the demonstrative **quickly** and **without sacrificing critical details**. This balance is crucial. If the demonstrative skews too heavily toward speed at the expense of supporting detail, the demonstrative will lack substance, thus lessening its impact. If it skews toward too much detail, sacrificing accessibility, the main point will be too obscure, again having a negative effect on its impact. A lawyer may have only seconds to make her point clear to the judge or jury. With a limited time frame, the lawyer's and witness's credibility may be impaired if the decision-maker senses that you have glossed over details. The judge and jurors may start to wonder what you are *not* showing them.

> "Once an initial impression is made, it is difficult to change."
>
> —Bradley Wine, litigation partner,
> Morrison & Foerster LLP

The following example was presented in trial by a defendant accused of failing to see financial red flags prior to making a loan. Just by glancing at the demonstrative, the differences in color and number of names in the two groups make it clear that they are dissimilar. The main point that almost no one saw a red flag is instantly recognizable, thus meeting the speed requirement.

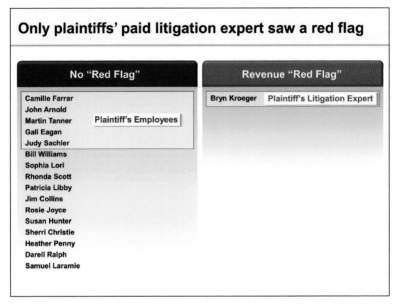

Figure 6—Lightning Speed Principle: Comparison

The demonstrative also has sufficient detail to back up the no "red flag" claim, satisfying the second Lightning Speed Principle requirement. The viewer can read the names of the witnesses who did and did not see any red flags. Digging further, the demonstrative shows that five of those witnesses were employees of the same plaintiff, making the "red flag" argument. And the crowning detail is that the only person who noticed that there was a red flag was the plaintiff's paid trial expert.

One way to employ the Lightning Speed Principle is to use icons, logos, illustrations, and pictures, which are forms of visual shorthand. If well-designed, well-placed, and used in moderation, they can increase mental processing speed. The advantage of quicker understanding is that the viewer can spend less time figuring out what your message is and more time digesting it. Images can orient and help remind the viewer what is being discussed.

As an example, take a look at the following two graphics regarding Tishman Speyer's and BlackRock's $6.3 billion purchase of Stuyvesant Town & Peter Cooper Village in New York City in 2006, which was financed in part by Commercial Backed Mortgage Securities (CBMS). The first example has only the text. While all of the information is there, it takes too much time to read and absorb, even if each piece of information is introduced one at a time. The relationships and interconnections are hard to see.

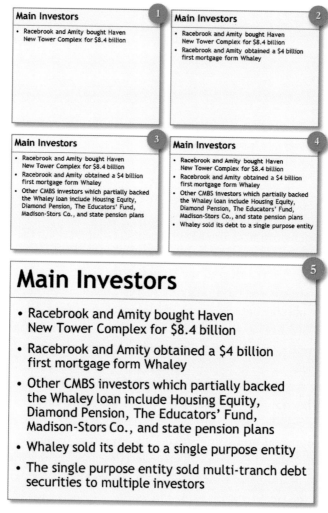

Figure 7—Lightning Speed Principle: Complex Process Before

Contrast that with the second example below, which has the identical information, but actually shows the interconnections and transactions and incorporates logos to reduce the amount of text. The movement of the process makes the information flow. And unlike with plain text, logos are familiar and may enable the viewer to remember the details better because he or she associates the logo with a party better than text. The images, arrows, and logos allow the viewer to focus on the transactions because the key players are readily discernible.

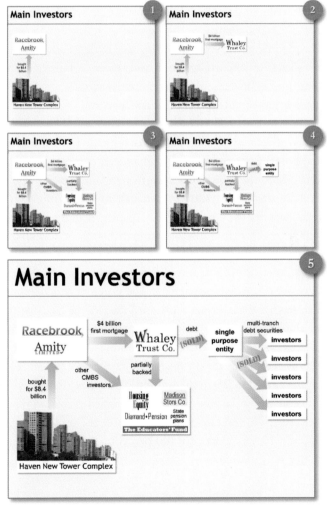

Figure 8—Lightning Speed Principle: Complex Process After

If you have the viewer's attention for only a few seconds and the viewer has to spend all of that time reading too much text, he or she may never understand your argument. On the other hand, if that reading time can be converted to processing time, the chance of your position being understood and believed increases. The use of visual shorthand is just one way to employ the Lightning Speed Principle.

Differential Emphasis

Differential Emphasis is the step of determining which data to emphasize, which data to display, and how to display it to make your point clearer and more persuasive. Advocacy design decisions regarding colors, text sizes, borders, background, and layout can direct the viewer's focus and make the demonstrative more persuasive.

Not every piece of data is relevant, and not every piece of data needs equal treatment. Being selective in what you show and how you show it—without being deceptive—is critical. For example, if you need to show events leading up to an alleged contract breach, it may not be necessary to show every communication between the parties. Or if it is, it may be necessary to break them down into smaller sub-timelines, keeping the amount of data displayed at any one time manageable. Or perhaps groupings or summaries of like data can make the timeline easier to understand.

A nice example of Differential Emphasis is from the "no red flag" contract case discussed on page 15. The point of this demonstrative was to show that the contract was signed despite the fact that the principal of the business was barely in the office, a bad fact for the other side. The calendar-type timeline incorporates several design devices intended to emphasize the prevalence of days out of the office. For the days on the calendars when she was out, the boxes are colored red and the font is bold. The date the contract was signed is colored yellow, also with bold text. For the days where she was in the office, the boxes are white. These design choices are 100 percent accurate while emphasizing the key information.

Figure 9—Differential Emphasis: Calendar Timeline

Another Differential Emphasis technique is showing the data in non-traditional ways. The following example compares the $125,969 in sales the plaintiff earned in 2002–2003 with those of the defendant, $58,781,232. The typical way to compare that data would be through the use of a bar graph, but this approach is problematic. If you plot those two sales figures in a bar graph, the differential is so great that you will end up with a tall bar for the defendant's sales and nothing perceptible for the plaintiff's sales. (Try it!) Even if the plaintiff's sales were perceptible—such as if the sales were $1 million—the bar graph that uses height as its only indication of the magnitude of the data set is not the most impactful way to emphasize the enormous difference in sales.

Showing the data in three dimensions ("3D")—height, width, and depth—instead of just height solves the practicality and effectiveness puzzles. Using depth, the stacks of cash (each representing $100,000) are arranged with some in back and others in front. The brain will interpret the stacks in back as reaching the bottom as opposed to floating at the point where they are visible. Using width occupies more of the visual real estate, further emphasizing the largesse of the defendant's sales, especially when compared to the plaintiff's. This is all the more impactful with having the cash spill over the right edge of the demonstrative. The same is true for height. The cash at the very top extends into the title bar area as opposed to having the title stay in the title bar and the content stay below. Breaking all of these design "rules" draws additional attention to the large difference in sales.

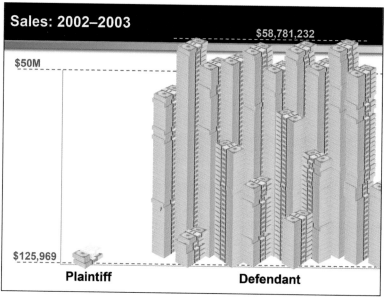

Figure 10—Differential Emphasis: Data Comparison in 3D

Because the preceding example is a representation of the cash total and not a mathematical graph, there are judges who might exclude this example under evidentiary rules because some of the stacks in back are not visible, despite the fact that they are implied. Accordingly, the leanings of a particular judge might dictate a more traditional approach. In such cases, it may be safer to design the demonstrative where the user can visually verify the figures being represented.

The demonstrative can be scaled back to incorporate only two dimensions ("2D")—height and width. Using bills each representing

$100,000, the viewer can add up the blocks and verify that the graphical representation of the plaintiff's and the defendant's sales matches the numerical. Although the 2D version is not quite as effective as the 3D version, it is still an acceptable alternative if the circumstance requires it.

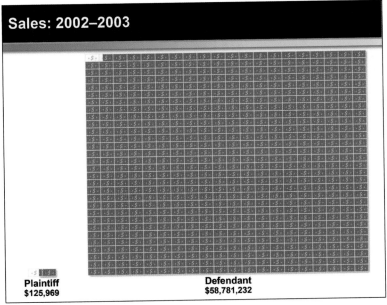

Figure 11—Differential Emphasis: Data Comparison in 2D

Advocacy Graphics

An advocacy graphic is when a demonstrative perfectly meshes the G➡S➡V Analysis with the three design principles just discussed. To see this in action, we should first look at an example that has the data to be an effective advocacy graphic, but is *not*. The following example is a graphic that was created by a client's in-house department that *attempts* to demonstrate to a lay audience the large number of jobs created throughout the United States by production of a particular lawnmower.

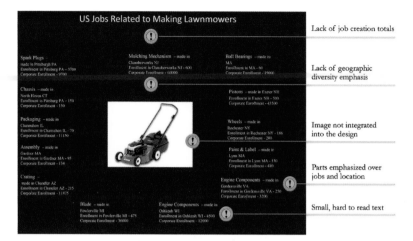

Figure 12—Ineffective Graphic

The design problems with this graphic include:

- The graphic totals neither the number of jobs for each location nor the total jobs throughout the United States.
- The graphic lists the locations of the jobs created by the product, but it is difficult to determine quickly if the impact is local, regional, or national.
- The product parts are listed before the locations and number of jobs, and are in a bigger font, which deemphasizes the most important data.
- The preceding issues are made worse by the small and hard-to-read serif font.
- The image of the product in the center with its white background is not integrated in the design, making it a distraction.

This is not an advocacy graphic, but there's hope! It can be turned into an advocacy graphic by applying G➡S➡V Analysis and the design principles of Know the User, Lightning Speed Principle, and Differential Emphasis.

G→S→V Analysis:

- **Goal:** The goal of this demonstrative is to show that the man-ufacturer of this product creates many jobs throughout the United States.
- **Strategy:** The strategy is to emphasize the number of jobs cre-ated in diverse locations, not the individual component parts or even the image of the product itself.
- **Visuals:** The visuals need to combine the data with a map to show geographic breadth with job creation totals.

Design Principles:

- **Know the User:** The user in this case is a jury. The visuals need to draw the jury's attention to the top line facts (lots of jobs with geographic diversity) despite the data-heavy information.
- **Lightning Speed Principle:** For speed, the visuals need to include a map so that the user can see the geographic diversity even if the user never even reads the location names. Perhaps more important is that it needs to include totals. The original has all of the raw data including both the corporate and manu-facturing jobs at each location but no local or national totals. Even with the main point leaping off of the page, as an advocacy graphic, it still needs the underlying location and job detail. Plus, using a larger sans serif font on a light background makes the data easier to read.
- **Differential Emphasis:** The totals and geographic diversity matter much more than the specific locations and the manu-facturing, corporate job split at each location, or an image of the product itself. The most noticeable object in the original is the product image. Then in the location text boxes, the name of the product part is in a large font and at the top, with every-thing else in a smaller font and below. The emphasis needs to be flipped. The job totals and geographic diversity have to be emphasized most while the remaining data and images need to be deemphasized.

The result is the following advocacy graphic.

Figure 13—Advocacy Graphic

Summary

Although these steps may seem burdensome, any experienced advocacy designer will perform most or all of them automatically. If the designer does not follow these steps, you are leaving the effectiveness of your demonstratives up to chance. You wouldn't permit that with the presentation of any other part of your case. The same goes for the most visible—and perhaps most attention-getting—part of your case. To summarize, the thought processes that must be used to create effective demonstratives are:

G➡S➡V Analysis:
- **Goal:** Why you are creating the demonstrative
- **Strategy:** The best way to create it
- **Visuals:** Creation using the three design principles

Design Principles:
- **Know the User:** Custom tailoring the demonstratives to the users of the information to maximize persuasion and impact
- **Lightning Speed Principle:** Communicating the main point or argument of the demonstrative quickly and without sacrificing detail
- **Differential Emphasis:** Determining which data to emphasize, which data to display, and how to display it to make your point clear and persuasive

An advocacy graphic is only as good as the thought and execution that goes into it. Graphics for graphics' sake are no more than a distraction. Graphics created analytically and methodically can help win over your audience. Thinking through the G➡S➡V Analysis is critical to success. Once complete, the three design principles—Know the User, Lightning Speed Principle, and Differential Emphasis—must all be taken into account. Following these principles will make your advocacy graphic a powerful and effective persuasion tool, which is the art of advocacy design.

"The art of advocacy is essential to the adversary system, and it is submitted that advocates should be encouraged to advocate, and to advocate effectively."

—Craig Spangenberg,
The Use of Demonstrative Evidence,
21 OHIO ST. L.J. 178, 189 (1960)

Demonstratives Practice

Planning and preparing demonstratives depends, in large part, on the phase of the case in which the demonstrative will be used. The following chapters endeavor, among other things, to show lawyers how demonstratives can be used during various phases of the case to persuade in (arguably) unconventional ways.

3

When Should Lawyers Begin Thinking about Demonstratives?

Right away.

Few lawyers these days would discount the role of demonstratives in persuading the finder of fact (in particular, jurors). In the authors' experience, however, most lawyers rarely consider demonstratives until late in the case, often when it is time to prepare for trial. By that time, however, fact and expert discovery are likely to have concluded, and the case themes must be chosen based on the evidence that was obtained without those themes in mind. Thinking about demonstratives early on—including the type of demonstrative evidence that will be powerful to persuade the finder of fact—expands the lawyer's ability to actually develop evidence supporting her themes, and not the other way around.

To be fair, demonstratives are sometimes used prior to trial—for example, in a brief or expert report. To the extent that is the case, those demonstratives are usually prepared at the last minute and without much care. This can lead to several problems—primarily that those demonstratives are often made in haste and are of poor quality, which can actually distract from the message being delivered. Even when the demonstratives are of respectable quality, they can nevertheless lead to inconsistent messaging if not clearly thought out (because if not clearly thought out, the demonstratives will evolve over the course of the case). In other words, the impression made with a demonstrative included in an early brief may be lost if that demonstrative has been retired by the time summary judgment motions are filed. Thinking about demonstratives early in the case, and including those demonstratives in briefs and expert reports, allows a lawyer to repeatedly expose the judge to the case themes with the hope of embedding those themes in the judge's mind. Moreover, because briefs and expert reports may become part of the record on appeal, having persuasive demonstratives in those documents can give a party a distinct advantage in persuading the court on appeal.

4

Using Demonstratives in Briefs

"Use a picture. It is worth a thousand words." A newspaper editor named Arthur Brisbane is often credited with first giving this advice in 1911,[1] suggesting to his reporters that words are not always adequate (or preferable) to get a point across.

The same advice is applicable to briefs. Demonstratives can be powerful argument enhancers. They can succinctly make a point that words cannot, particularly when complex information is being conveyed. Demonstratives can also, importantly, make the brief more interesting and capture the judge's attention. Research indicates that people often remember things they see better than things they hear. As a result, when used in conjunction with words, demonstratives can make an argument more memorable (and perhaps improve that argument's chances if the other party gets the last word).

Yet most lawyers do not use demonstratives in briefs. (It is probably more accurate to say most lawyers do not *think* to use them.)

---

1. William Safire has provided an alternate explanation of the origin of this phrase. *See* William Safire, *On Language; Worth a Thousand Words*, THE N.Y. TIMES MAGAZINE (Apr. 7, 1996), *available at* www.nytimes.com/1996/04/07/magazine/on-language-worth-a-thousand-words. html.

Anecdotal evidence suggests that many of these lawyers think that legal briefs are no place for hifalutin pictures and may not be received well by a judge. To the contrary, a number of judges have stated that demonstratives in briefs are more than welcome. A couple of examples:

- "I just want to put in a plug for diagrams, photographs, charts, and other graphic ways of communicating. Everything doesn't have to be communicated with long sentences. Some things are better done through graphs."[2]
- "I think that any form of demonstrative evidence that is going to speed the process by which the court is going to understand what you are saying makes great sense. I mean, you know the adage a picture is worth a thousand words, sometimes these charts and other forms of demonstrative evidence are very, very useful. . . . And we are seeing an increasing use, at least I am, especially in patent cases, of technicolor inserts, photographs and things like that in the briefs that are very helpful, at least to me."[3]

Skeptical lawyers should also keep in mind that the same judges who are reading their briefs are constantly bombarded with information in the form of graphics. Major newspapers, including the *New York Times*, *Wall Street Journal*, and *USA Today*, regularly include graphics (sometimes referred to as "infographics") to summarize, support, or explain the news they report. Why? Because they recognize that sometimes words alone are not sufficient.

To be sure, not all arguments require demonstrative support, and many arguments do not benefit from demonstratives at all. Indeed, some lawyers are guilty of overusing demonstratives when mere words would suffice. It cannot be overstated that careful consideration and

---

2. Judge Paul R. Michel, U.S. Court of Appeals for the Federal Circuit, *Remarks, Sixteenth Annual Judicial Conference of the United States Court of Appeals for the Federal Circuit*, 193 F.3d 177, 199 (1993).
3. Judge Raymond Clevenger, U.S. Court of Appeals for the Federal Circuit, *Ten Commandments for Appellate Briefing*, discussed in Rachel C. Hughey, *Effective Appellate Advocacy Before The Federal Circuit: A Former Law Clerk's Perspective*, 11 J. OF APP. PRAC. & PROC. 401 (2010).

judgment should be used when determining whether demonstratives will improve an argument—or if they will only serve to detract from the point being made.

There are many ways that demonstratives can be used to improve the understandability or persuasiveness of a brief. Perhaps the most fundamental way to use a demonstrative is to show the court what the dispute is actually about, particularly if the details of the case are not commonly known. For example, assume that the case is about a particular type of corkscrew (for removing wine corks) called a "rabbit" corkscrew. The judge may not know what a rabbit corkscrew is, or perhaps has seen that type of corkscrew but not know what it is called. Regardless, it is in the lawyer's best interest to ensure that the judge becomes familiar with a rabbit corkscrew, so that the judge has all of the tools necessary to understand the argument. Thus, as shown in the following example, an image of a rabbit corkscrew can be included in the brief alongside a description of the device.

This case involves a specific type of corkscrew called a "rabbit" corkscrew, so-called because the device resembles a rabbit. Seen below, the rabbit corkscrew works through a combination of pressure grips and a lever that permit a user to easily insert the auger (what most people understand as the "corkscrew") into 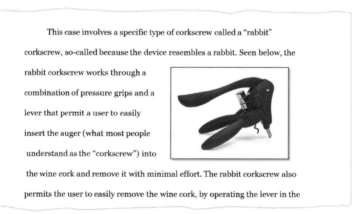 the wine cork and remove it with minimal effort. The rabbit corkscrew also permits the user to easily remove the wine cork, by operating the lever in the

Figure 14—Examples of Demonstratives in Briefs:
Visual Depiction of an Object

A lawyer can also use a diagram that is color coded to delineate the various components of a device, as seen in the next figure. This type of demonstrative may be applicable in a products liability or patent infringement case to educate the judge about the product or patent at issue. The primary purpose of this demonstrative is generally to visually indicate the different components of the device. It can also be used, however, to show that certain components are distinct (by using contrasting colors) or that the components are related (by using similar colors).

The asserted patent is invalid because each of the elements of the asserted claims are found in the prior art. As seen in Figure 1 of the Smith reference, for example, the prior art disclosed a device for removing a wine cork that having a handle (blue), an auger (grey), and an extraction lever (yellow). These prior-art elements are identical to the limitations recited in the asserted claims. When viewed in conjunction with the other prior-art devices disclosing a similar mechanism

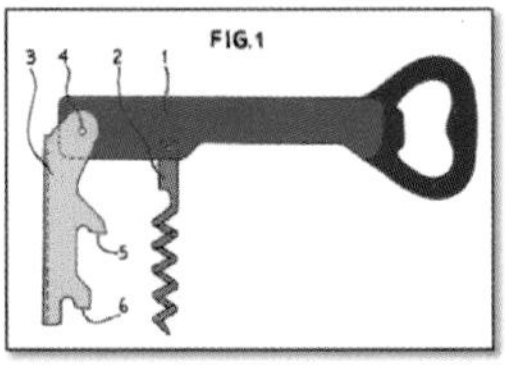

Figure 15—Examples of Demonstratives in Briefs:
Identifying Components Using Color

Similarly, demonstratives can be used to identify the different components of an actual device or mechanism that does not lend itself to color coding. In the next example, the various components of a bottle opener are labeled. This type of demonstrative will help to familiarize the judge with the terminology used in the case, and may serve as a handy (and easy-to-find) reference if the judge encounters unfamiliar terminology elsewhere in the briefs.

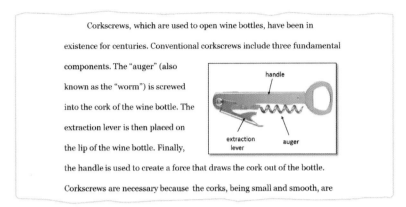

Figure 16—Examples of Demonstratives in Briefs: Annotated Illustration

Demonstratives are often effective to show a timeline or a series of key events. Simply put, many people are visual learners, and seeing events identified in a timeline can provide important context about how events relate to other events. For example, timelines can be particularly effective when showing that certain events are far apart or that one event triggered another.

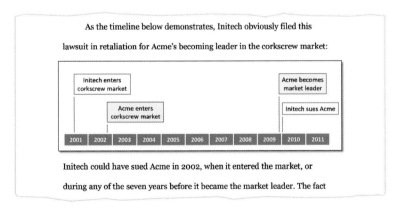

Figure 17—Examples of Demonstratives in Briefs: Timeline

Timelines can also be effective to show that certain events or occurrences are clustered together (e.g., an industrial accident resulting in higher incidence of cancer in a small town), timing of core facts in relation to external events, frequency of events, etc.

Likewise, demonstratives can be particularly effective to show the similarities or differences between two things. In the following example below, demonstratives are used to show that the alleged infringing bottle opener on the right is unlike the bottle opener described in the patent.

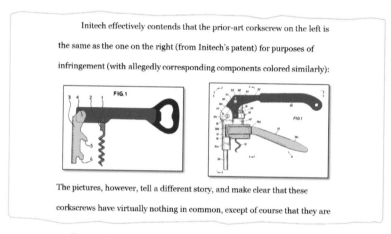

Initech effectively contends that the prior-art corkscrew on the left is the same as the one on the right (from Initech's patent) for purposes of infringement (with allegedly corresponding components colored similarly):

The pictures, however, tell a different story, and make clear that these corkscrews have virtually nothing in common, except of course that they are

Figure 18—Examples of Demonstratives in Briefs:
Component Similarities or Differences

Demonstratives are also useful for emphasizing a particular part of a document, particularly if it relates to a key fact or admission. Skeptics may say that they can simply tell the judge what the document says. True enough. But seeing the document speak for itself can be more persuasive (and draw more attention) than burying the fact or admission in the text where it looks like, and can get lost among, all of the other words.

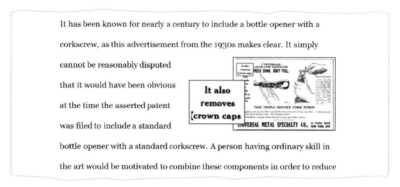

Figure 19—Examples of Demonstratives in Briefs: Document Call-Out

A word about formatting demonstratives in briefs. When a demonstrative in a brief is significantly narrower than the width of a line of text, it is best to avoid placing graphics in-line with text. If not, the result is distracting dead space on the page and does not look aesthetically pleasing.

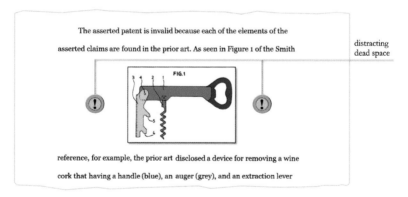

Figure 20—Formatting Demonstratives in Briefs—Avoid:
Narrow Image In-Line with Text

When feasible, it is best for the text to wrap around the image, in the same way that images are formatted in books and newspapers. This formatting looks more professional and also minimizes the amount of space taken up by the image (thereby giving you more words if you are constrained by page limits). The following example looks better than the previous in-line example and provides substantial space for additional words on the page. To apply this formatting in Microsoft Word, right-click on the image and use the "Square" or "Tight" option under the "Wrap Text" context menu. To apply the formatting used in Figure 21 below, use the "Top and Bottom" option.

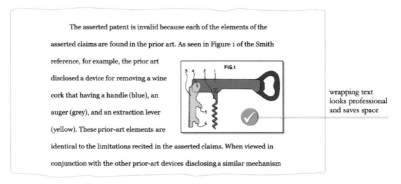

Figure 21—Formatting Demonstratives in Briefs—Preferable:
Wrapping Text Around the Image

Briefs can have demonstratives incorporated into the text and also attached as exhibits. The same brief can have both as in the two following examples from a trademark case. The first example, comparing different logos, was embedded in the text of the brief.

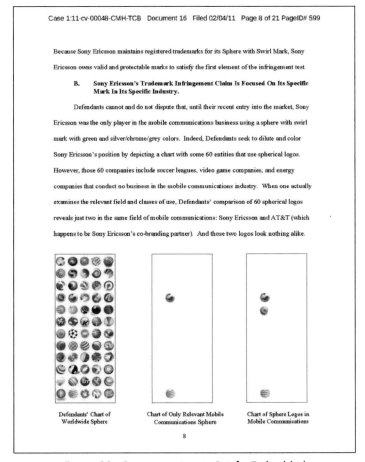

Figure 22—Demonstratives in Briefs: Embedded

The second example shows the geographic expansion of service over time. It takes up an entire page and therefore was attached as an exhibit to the brief.

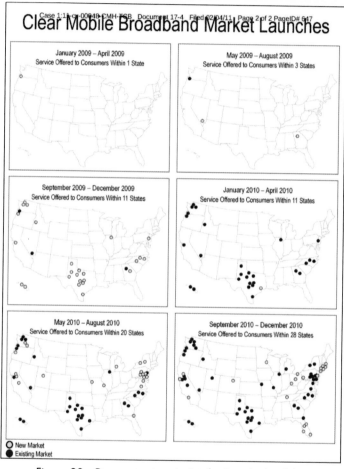

Figure 23—Demonstratives in Briefs: Attached Exhibit

5

Using Demonstratives in Expert Reports

Expert witnesses are often the keystone of a lawyer's case. Experts are able to credibly explain why a product was not the cause of an injury, why a patent is not infringed, or how much money is necessary to make a plaintiff whole. Good expert witnesses are teachers, and teachers use demonstratives to aid in the learning process. Because an expert report is a written document, the ways that demonstratives can be used in an expert report are similar to how demonstratives can be used in briefs, as discussed in Chapter Four.

Thinking carefully about demonstratives in expert reports is important for several reasons. For example, using demonstratives in expert reports forces the lawyer to think about case themes and how the evidence may ultimately be presented at trial. Having the expert involved in preparing the demonstratives will help shape case themes and ensure that the demonstratives to be used at trial are prepared correctly. A demonstrative used at trial will be more credible if it appears in the expert's report and if the expert can testify that she participated in its creation.

Perhaps more importantly, the effective use of demonstratives in an expert report can bolster the expert's report and testimony. As is the case with briefs, demonstratives often can make a point that words cannot, in addition to making the expert's report more interesting.

Although many lawyers think of expert reports as merely a disclosure document or a "deposition handbook" to aid the expert during deposition, it is not unusual for an expert report to be submitted to the court in connection with summary judgment motions (if a declaration is not prepared) or in connection with a motion to exclude the expert under *Daubert*. Consider the situation, for example, that your adversary has submitted your expert's report in connection with a *Daubert* motion. While of course the words of the report and credentials of the report are paramount, a professional expert report with professional graphics will only increase your chances of success. And because a picture is worth a thousand words, demonstratives in an expert report may be viewed as disclosing more than the words themselves, thus giving the expert's lawyer an edge in disputes about whether an expert's report discloses this or that.

As already suggested, it is important that demonstratives in an expert's report are carefully thought through. If the demonstratives in an expert report do not line up with the demonstratives used at trial— e.g., in terms of color-coding, visual appearance of important graphics, commonality of themes, etc.—then the demonstratives in the expert report have the potential to create confusion if the expert relies on, or is impeached by, using her expert report.

6

Using Demonstratives in Depositions

Use of demonstratives in depositions is somewhat uncommon in the authors' experience. Demonstratives, however, can serve several important purposes in that setting. For example, using a timeline helps a witness piece together different events and reduce the likelihood of the witness misremembering. Using a demonstrative map during a deposition may help the witness provide facts about where something happened.

Consider a lawsuit that alleges wrongful death, where the plaintiff's husband was electrocuted by an allegedly faulty toaster, and the plaintiff's eyewitness testimony is necessary to establish that it was not her husband's own negligence that caused his death. A critical issue may be whether she was actually in a location in the house where she could observe the electrocution. In that case, a demonstrative like the one that follows could prove extremely useful in determining precisely where she was, whether her vantage point from that location enabled her to see the unfortunate turn of events, etc.

Once a demonstrative has been used in a deposition, it may carry additional persuasive weight when it is subsequently used at trial, particularly if, such as in the following figure, the witness can be made to annotate the exhibit. For example, the plaintiff can be asked to mark an "X" to indicate where she was standing when her husband was electrocuted.

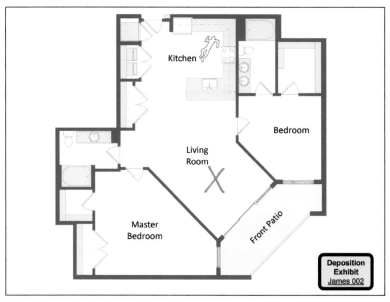

Figure 24—Demonstratives in Depositions: Map Annotated by Deponent

Perhaps the defendant in this same case obtained the medical records of the plaintiff's husband. Defense counsel may prepare a timeline that summarizes different medical events and have relevant witnesses give deposition testimony verifying those facts in the timeline presented to them. When the events in the timeline are derived from documents, the documents should be introduced as deposition exhibits. A potentially powerful tool, as in the example that follows, is to combine timeline events with the corresponding documents. At trial or hearing, a timeline such as this can be hyperlinked, where clicking on the document thumbnail will pull up the full document and key call-out.

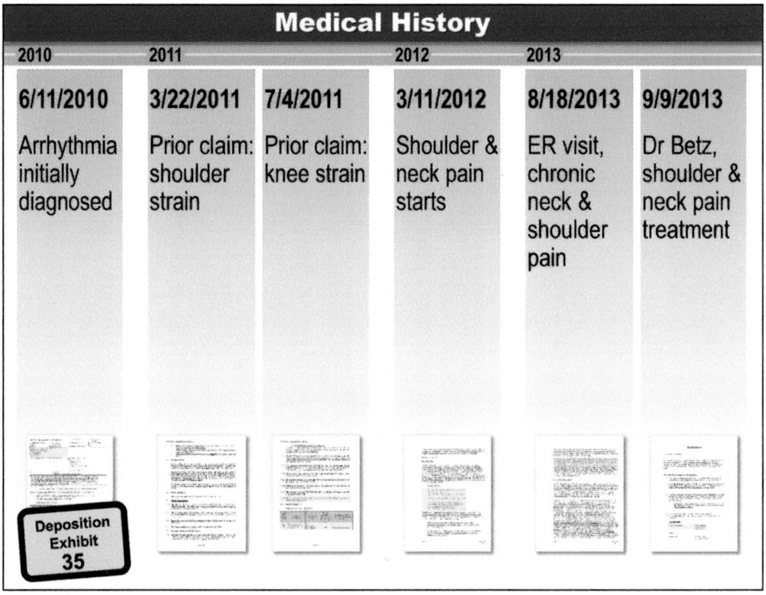

Medical History					
2010	**2011**		**2012**	**2013**	
6/11/2010	**3/22/2011**	**7/4/2011**	**3/11/2012**	**8/18/2013**	**9/9/2013**
Arrhythmia initially diagnosed	Prior claim: shoulder strain	Prior claim: knee strain	Shoulder & neck pain starts	ER visit, chronic neck & shoulder pain	Dr Betz, shoulder & neck pain treatment

Deposition Exhibit 35

Figure 25—Demonstratives in Depositions: Timeline and Relevant Documents Verified by Deponent

7

Using Demonstratives at Trial

Trial is the one phase of a case where virtually all litigators will be familiar with the use of demonstratives. Building on the knowledge and experience most litigators are likely to have, this chapter endeavors to provide time-tested guidelines for effective use of demonstratives at trial.[1]

Opening Statements

Opening statements are supposed to provide a high-level overview of the case and introduce the fact finder to the themes of the case. Notably, most judges will not permit the parties to show the jury actual evidence unless it has already been admitted, so demonstratives can be particularly helpful during opening statements to preview what the lawyers think the evidence will show. This can include explanation of any technology at issue, introduction to the party's witnesses, timelines of key events, and if the court allows it, the content of pre-admitted

---

1. Much of what is discussed in this chapter is equally applicable to hearings.

exhibits. It is important, when preparing opening demonstratives, to think through how those demonstratives will play a role during the trial as the evidence is presented, so that the themes presented during the opening perpetuate and are consistent through trial.

Witnesses

A properly prepared exhibit will help highlight the key points of a witness's testimony and can enhance the credibility of that witness. Demonstratives are typically used to support expert testimony and are less common with fact witnesses. When they are used with fact witnesses, the most typical types of demonstratives are pre-made document call-outs and timelines—all issues related to underlying facts in the case.

When creating demonstratives for use with expert witnesses, it is important for those demonstratives to be consistent—in terms of color, look and feel, and messaging—with the lawyer's other trial demonstratives. If not, there is risk of confusing the fact finder or looking unprepared—all of which harm the credibility and persuasiveness of the expert (and the party that expert represents). Typical expert demonstratives include graphics and animation used to explain underlying technological concepts, charts, tables, document call-outs, and sometimes bullet points.

Regarding bullet points, it is virtually impossible for most lawyers to prepare demonstratives without text. There is nothing inherently wrong with including text in a demonstrative, but there is a fine line between an acceptable amount of text and too much. A confident witness may be able to remember and provide her testimony with a textless demonstrative. A nervous witness, on the other hand, may need some help, and a demonstrative with bullet points can go a long way toward enabling the witness to remember and give her testimony. This latter option must be used with caution; if it looks like the witness is just reading the slide, it may give the impression that the lawyer is telling the witness what to say, and the witness's credibility could be harmed as a result. (*See* section titled "Bullet Lists" in Chapter 14.)

Closing Statements

Closing statements are the lawyer's opportunity to summarize the evidence and persuade the jury to find in his favor. The demonstratives shown during closing statements, whether they are key document callouts, timelines, maps, or illustrations, should in most cases already be familiar to the judge and jury from their use during the trial. Just as with the words spoken at closing, everything that is introduced visually is meant to reinforce what the lawyer has already taught. An exception to this guideline is the use of demonstratives that highlight critical trial testimony. Pairing trial testimony with an image of the witness can be a powerful reminder of who provided the testimony and how that witness fits into the case, which can be especially important in longer cases with many witnesses. Following is an example of such a testimony demonstrative.

The key witness doesn't know what happened

John Smith

Q. Isn't it true you were not at home when the accident happened?

A. Yes.

Q. So you can't say for sure what actually happened?

A. I guess not.

Trial testimony page 13, lines 3-8

Figure 26—Demonstratives in Closing Statements:
Stylized Testimony and Photo

Think strategically instead of leaping into making demonstratives. Every demonstrative must mesh with your facts, arguments, trial themes, etc. The Goal ➡ Strategy ➡ Visuals (G➡S➡V) Analysis detailed in Chapter Two runs the attorney though a thoughtful process for making demonstratives, instead of making graphics for graphics' sake or making demonstratives for every conceivable issue, argument, document, analogy, etc. Be purposeful and selective.

Make sure you really need a slide. Attorneys often go overboard when preparing demonstratives for trial. As suggested elsewhere in this book, however, increasing the number of demonstratives does not necessarily result in increased persuasiveness.

In fact, demonstratives have a real potential to distract from the argument itself. For example, research shows that people read text-heavy slides instead of listening to the presenter and then their brain shuts down until the next slide. This is obviously not ideal, where the focus should be on the attorney or the witness who is speaking.

Demonstratives can also rob the attorney of a way of interacting with the jury. For example, displaying a previously prepared document "call-out" of an exhibit can be far less interactive and engaging than simply talking the jury through the important parts of an exhibit using the exhibit itself, either with a document camera (commonly referred to as an "ELMO") or with trial presentation software such as Sanction, TrialDirector, OnCue, etc.

Demonstratives are meant to aid an argument. Keep that in mind as you go about preparing them.

Trim your timelines. Almost every case with demonstratives has at least one timeline. Timelines are great tools to tell a story in a condensed and succinct fashion, but it is easy to defeat the purpose by adding too much detail. Overloading a timeline is a natural instinct since they are usually created not too long before trial, when attorneys are focused on every last piece of evidence that supports their case. The result is an ineffective timeline resulting from too many entries or too much text.

Think of it this way: save your multi-page recitation of events for your briefing, and extract only those facts for your timeline that you would use in an "elevator pitch." What if you had only one minute to describe the core events supporting your case? No matter how big the case, how many parties, how complicated the facts, every case can and should be boiled down to a handful of key events. This does not mean that you have to sacrifice detail in the presentation of your case. Just keep in mind that a timeline is a high-level summary of your best facts.

Maximize your design resources. It is common for lawyers to inefficiently utilize graphic advocacy designers. For example, "Turn this brief into a PowerPoint" is a common request. While this work order will certainly remove demonstratives from a lawyer's plate, albeit temporarily, it is not an optimal way to create a demonstrative. First, the resulting initial draft of the work product will inevitably leave a lot to be desired. By asking for such a conversion without providing any guidance, the lawyer is in effect delegating the work of lawyers to designers. It is also not fair. To do their work, designers need to know about the case, the case themes, and the lawyer's goals for the demonstratives. Without this context, the designers cannot do what they do best: create demonstratives that will aid the lawyer's argument and appeal to a jury. Asking a designer to create demonstratives without context will lead to less impactful demonstratives.

To avoid this result, give the designers context, ideally through a meeting to discuss the case and purpose of the demonstratives. This approach also gives the lawyers an important asset: someone who can provide a fresh perspective—one closer to that of the jury's—and speak to whether or not the arguments and proposed or accompanying demonstratives are effective.

A lawyer should also be specific about what he or she wants, while at the same time recognizing that the designer should be allowed to do their job. Providing the designer with examples the attorney has seen and liked in the past (or such as those in the Inspiration Index accompanying this book) can go a long way toward eliminating unnecessary rounds of draft slides. It may be helpful to ask the designer to provide several options of a particular demonstrative for the attorney to choose from.

Make sure your slides look the same. A party's presentation at trial should be consistent. Sometimes, however, there is disharmony among the demonstratives used by different attorneys on the same team because they are not talking to each other as demonstratives are prepared. Inconsistent messaging and formatting can distract and possibly confuse the jurors. One person on a trial team, presumably the lead lawyer, should have control over the direction of the slides and the ultimate say on the themes to be presented.

Make sure your demonstratives are not overly complicated. This rule is especially important if the demonstratives are meant for a jury. Experience shows that many attorneys find it impossible to make slides simple enough for the average person. But it is not so much about the intelligence of the audience as it is the fact that neither the judge nor jury has invested months or years learning about the case like the attorneys have. One way to ensure that the slides are not overly complicated is to try not to include every aspect of your argument on a slide. Again, a demonstrative is meant to aid an argument, not to make the argument on its own. Save some material for the accompanying testimony or argument. It will improve your presentation.

Consider whether you really need an animation. Animations are often popular because they have the "whiz bang" factor. Before requesting or using an animation, however, consider whether you really need it. Animations can be helpful in certain circumstances, and in some cases they are indispensable. One major problem with animations, however, and particularly with very short animations, is that the judge and/or jurors need to be focused on the screen for the few seconds when the key part of the animation occurs. If they are not looking, then the demonstrative cannot make its point. One exception can be a "looping" animation, which plays continuously over and over again. These, in some cases, can be helpful to convey how something operates when a static demonstrative will not do.

Make sure your demonstratives are accurate. Make sure everything in your demonstrative is correct. Then double-check it. And then have someone with fresh eyes review the demonstrative with the same goal in mind. Many a fabulous demonstrative has been totally discredited because a silly mistake opened them (through the sponsoring witness) up to cross-examination. Relatedly, make absolutely sure your demonstrative is not misleading.

The following example shows how data that is true can, nonetheless, be displayed in a deceptive fashion. This bar chart makes the $2.5 million difference in revenue look quite large by eliminating the revenue from $0 to $149,999,999.

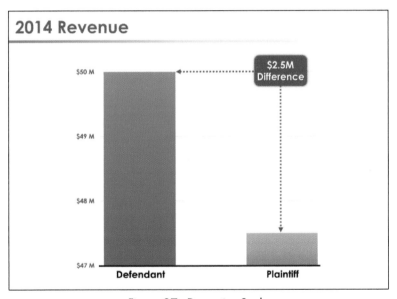

Figure 27—Deceptive Scale

The very same data shown on a full scale, however, shows quite a different picture. With the corrected scale, the relative difference is not significant under the circumstances.

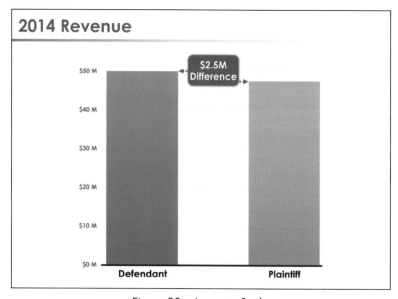

Figure 28—Accurate Scale

A single misleading slide can cause you, your client, and your witness to lose credibility with the fact finder.

Make sure your demonstrative conveys the message that you think it conveys. Like infographics of the type found in major newspapers, the underlying concept sought to be conveyed by most demonstratives should be capable of being understood within a few seconds without substantial explanation. *Figure 9—Differential Emphasis: Calendar Timeline,*[2] for example, shows clearly that the person was rarely in the office during the time period when the contract was signed. *Figure 10—Differential Emphasis: Data Comparison in 3D*[3] and *Figure 11—*

2. *See* page 19, *supra.*
3. *See* page 20, *supra.*

Differential Emphasis: Data Comparison in 2D[4] make clear that the defendant's sales were vastly higher than the plaintiff's sales.

An attorney who has lived and breathed the case for years already knows the information that is supposed to be conveyed by the slide and thus is often a poor judge of whether the demonstrative does a good job. Best practice requires having someone without a strong connection to the case review the demonstrative for this purpose. The best-case scenario is to conduct a mock trial and have a mock jury evaluate the slides in the context of the arguments and themes that will be presented at trial. If a mock trial is not feasible, however, simply showing the demonstrative to people who are unfamiliar with the case—e.g., legal secretaries, family members, etc.—can provide a lot of information about whether the demonstrative will perform as intended.

Make sure you have a demonstrative exchange set up. The court will almost always establish a time and procedure for exchanging demonstratives. In the rare case when this does not happen, strongly consider agreeing to a procedure and schedule with the other side, making a joint proposal to the court. It is better to iron out any objections to the demonstratives with opposing counsel and the court before they are shown in court. While doing so will eliminate the "surprise" factor that so many attorneys are fond of, it will also eliminate the possibility that you are embarrassed when the judge does not permit you to use a key demonstrative, which if previously vetted could have been amended to accommodate opposing counsel's objections. Depending on what was shown and if there was a jury, there is even potential for larger negative impact on the case, such as a mistrial if the demonstrative was highly objectionable or inflammatory.

Use an opposing party's demonstratives against them. Another benefit of a demonstrative exchange is that it gives you the opportunity to use the other side's demonstratives against them. An effective way to do this is to annotate the opposing counsel's demonstratives to show

---

4. *See* page 21, *supra.*

how they are incorrect, misleading, etc. For example, see the following demonstrative, which points out the deceptive scale in Figure 27, *supra*, assuming it wasn't already excluded by the judge.

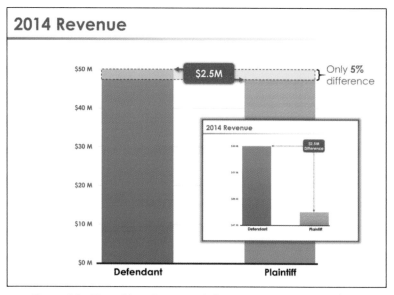

Figure 29—Using Your Opponent's Demonstratives against Them

Save your "gotcha" material. A downside of the (still necessary) demonstrative exchange is that there is rarely a good opportunity to create demonstratives with the "gotcha" material you think your adversary may not know about. Also, just as you can try to use the other side's demonstratives against them, rest assured that they have the same intentions for your demonstratives. In the end, make sure the demonstratives you make are as impervious as possible to attack. And keep your best impeachment material in your back pocket. Good impeachment does not always require a demonstrative.

When a demonstrative is not a demonstrative. The typical demonstrative of a document call-out is, like all other demonstratives, subject to the demonstrative exchange, thus giving the other side advance warning. This is because most document call-outs have some type of inherent "argument," addition, characterization, etc. The demonstrative nature of it—making it an aid to argument—may be something as subtle as the use of a color or a seemingly neutral title. Consider the example that follows. The color in the title bar is likely the color theme used by the party that created it. The title font also has the same potential. Maybe they are the same color and font that were used in the company's logo. In addition, while seemingly innocuous, the title itself identifies the aspect of the email that the attorneys would like to draw attention to. There is no bombast in the demonstrative, but it still has characteristics that detract from its neutrality.

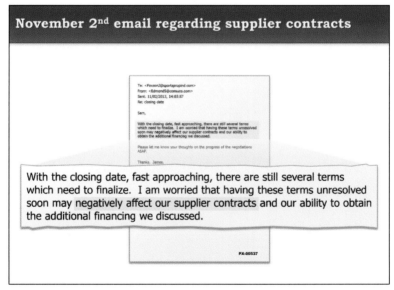

Figure 30—Typical Document Call-Out

If there are call-outs that you want to keep close to the vest, then refer to the previous rule about making sure you really need a slide. The following graphic shows what would be on screen if the call-out was created on-the-fly with trial presentation software such as Sanction, TrialDirector, or OnCue. The substance of the graphic is nearly identical to the prior example, except that it lacks a word-smithed title and instead has just the exhibit number. Because it is created on-the-fly, there is no demonstrative to be exchanged, and thus it preserves the potential for surprise. Perhaps more importantly, using trial presentation software requires the attorney to walk through the document step-by-step, thereby providing some context before calling the fact finder's attention to the critical passage. This will make the presentation more interactive and the point more understandable.

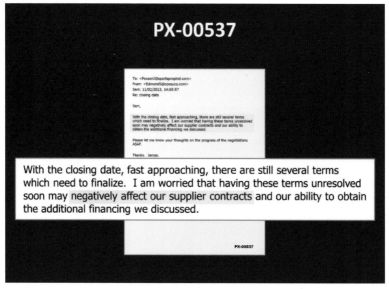

Figure 31—Call-Out Made Using Trial Presentation Software

Demonstratives Visual Encyclopedia

The following Visual Encyclopedia or "style guide" has examples of different types and styles of demonstratives. It provides examples of what different demonstrative types and styles may look like and serves as a best practices guide. Nonetheless, every case and every trial team are different. Let your facts, the law, and your creativity be your guide as to what works best for your case.

8

General Demonstrative Design

The majority of electronic demonstratives are created in Microsoft PowerPoint, but it is not the only software in play. Other programs commonly used are Apple's presentation software Keynote, Adobe's Creative Suite, various trial presentation software (e.g., Sanction, TrialDirector, OnCue, etc.), tablet apps, and video editing software. In creating effective demonstratives, the software platform is not as important as what you do with it.

Overall Design

In designing your demonstratives, what matters most is getting your message out. The design is the vehicle for getting there. When a demonstrative suffers from "design abuse," the results are never good. As an example, the core issue with the following demonstrative is that the design, such as it is, overpowers the message.

Figure 32—General Demonstrative Design—Overall: Mistakes to Avoid

To make the message more prominent than the design, some general rules to follow include:

- Use the standard 4:3 slide ratio (aligns with most court AV systems and sizes better on paper)
- High-contrast decorative slide elements and bullets are distracting
- Use bright yellows and reds sparingly
- Use sentence-case type for most effective readability
- Always avoid all-caps
- Limit font types
- Don't apply drop shadows to dark-colored text
- Lock height and width ratios on images to avoid distortions
- Keep footers small and subtle

Applying these principles to the information in the prior example could end up with something more like the following demonstrative, which makes the main point that the bottle opener has a unique feature. "But hold on, where are the bullets?" you might ask. Ah, good question. You can just say them. If your graphic does not make your point clear, adding words is not necessarily the cure. A better designed demonstrative is likely what you need. If you really need to, put the bullet points in the notes section so you remember to make them. If you absolutely, positively need bullet points in your demonstrative, consider using the least number of words possible in a distraction-free and easy-to-read font.

Figure 33—General Demonstrative Design—Overall: Clean Design

Color

Color Scheme

The overall color scheme can set the tone of the demonstrative. Depending on the specific design, dark tones with a light-colored font could signal a bold, aggressive stance as in the next example. One thing to note is that dark backgrounds require more boxes for text and images, which has the potential to increase the amount of visual clutter.

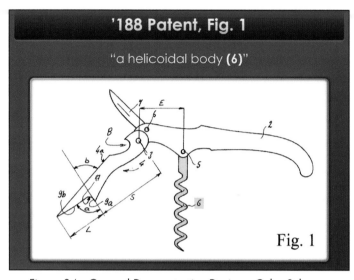

Figure 34—General Demonstrative Design—Color Scheme:
Dark Tones and Light Font

Soft, light tones with a darker font can have a warmer feel. Although less "aggressive" in feel, lighter tones can have a cleaner look with less need for boxes. Compare this example with the previous one.

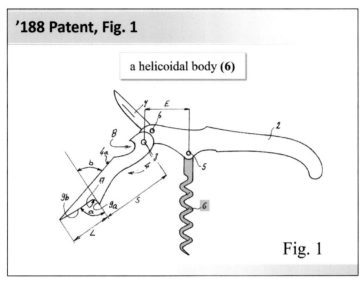

Figure 35—General Demonstrative Design—Color Scheme:
Light Tones and Dark Font

As with many demonstrative design decisions, there are not necessarily "right" or "wrong" decisions. Regardless, it is key to understand the potential impacts of those choices.

Color Messaging

Colors can be used for drawing attention. Bold, bright colors that stand out from the general color scheme generally work well. As in the "clean design" example in Figure 33, the red "Notice this" text with the leader and circle draw the viewers' attention to those elements.

Colors also have a messaging component. The following colors can have the following associated messages:

- **Red:** stop, bad, loss
- **Green:** go, good, profit
- **Yellow:** caution, alert

Figure 36—General Demonstrative Design—Color Messaging:
Light Tones and Dark Font

Although red, green, and yellow tend to have those messaging associations, it does not have to be the case. As with all things demonstrative, it depends on how they are used. Not only that, there are times when you explicitly should use or conversely do not want to use particular colors for messaging. One reason to potentially use or avoid a particular color is when it could be associated with your client. For example, if a client's logo is red, using that color to signal "bad" could work cross-purposes by also associating "bad" with the client.

Color Vision Deficiency ("Color Blindness")

Another consideration regarding color choice is the issue of color vision deficiency, commonly called color blindness.[1] While there is almost no way to know if any jurors are color blind, it is possible to learn if judges, arbitrators, mediators, and the like are color blind. The most common color blindness combination is having difficulty distinguishing between different shades of red and green. The next figure shows what red and green look like to someone with typical vision (swatches on the left) and red/green color blindness (swatches on the right).

....Red and green swatches   ....Red and green swatches if color blind

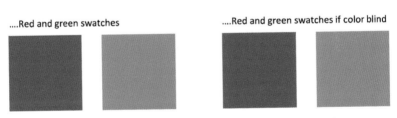

Figure 37—General Demonstrative Design—Color Vision Deficiency:
Red/Green "Color Blindness"

There is also blue/yellow color blindness, but it is less common. An even rarer condition is achromatopsia or complete color-blindness where people can only see things as black and white or in shades of

---

1. The authors obtained information on color vision deficiency from *Color Vision Deficiency*, American Optometric Association, www.aoa.org/patients-and-public/eye-and-vision-problems/glossary-of-eye-and-vision-conditions/color-deficiency?sso=y.

gray. If you find this, it is imperative to take that information into account when making color choices. Even if you don't know, you may be well-served by using other distinguishing design features in addition to color—and this doesn't just mean add more text. A few design examples would be using a dashed line different from solid lines, different shaped boxes, different placement, and the like.

Figure 38—General Demonstrative Design—Color Vision Deficiency:
"Color Blindness" Work-Arounds

9

Call-Outs

Document call-outs may be the most ubiquitous form of demonstrative. Nearly every case has some core set of documents that are key to the case outcome. Showing the key provisions of those documents in a compelling way can make memorable the most important points of the most important documents. There are many ways to make call-outs. Depending on the look and overall atmospherics that are part of the strategy of any particular case, a trial team can choose the right call-out style for the right case.

Call-Out Types

Depending on the aesthetic you are looking for and the theme you are establishing (simple and clear, straight from the evidence, etc.), different call-out types can be deployed. There are three basic call-out types: box, torn/ripped page, and retyped. *See* the section titled "Call-Out Layouts," *infra* in this chapter, which illustrates different layouts for these call-out types.

Box Call-Out

The box call-out is the most common. As its name suggests, it is a call-out in a box.

Corkscrew with double propping lever, with an adjacent extraction cork-screw, in which the double propping lever presents a first base lever hinged which one end to the handle of the tool, and a second extension lever for the propping hinged at the end of said first base lever, whereby said second extension lever for the propping presents two propping support teeth, one support teeth at the end and one support teeth close to its articulation to the print base lever.

Figure 39—Call-Outs: Box

Torn/Ripped Page Call-Out

The torn/ripped page call-out is a call-out in a box designed to look like it is torn straight from the page, giving it a more authentic look. It also visually suggests that the text called out is only an excerpt.

Corkscrew with double propping lever, with an adjacent extraction cork-screw, in which the double propping lever presents a first base lever hinged which one end to the handle of the tool, and a second extension lever for the propping hinged at the end of said first base lever, whereby said second extension lever for the propping presents two propping support teeth, one support teeth at the end and one support teeth close to its articulation to the print base lever.

Figure 40—Call-Outs: Torn Page

Retyped Call-Out

The potentially least authentic looking call-out is the retyped call-out. Nonetheless, there are several reasons why it may be warranted. Sometimes the image quality of the source document is so poor that the only way to reasonably read it is if the text is retyped. Another common reason is if the call-out text in the source document is very wide with a small font; to have it fit the demonstrative without changing the aspect ratio could make the text tiny. A legible retyped call-out is always better than an "original" illegible one.

Corkscrew with double propping lever, with an adjacent extraction cork-screw, in which the double propping lever presents a first base lever hinged which one end to the handle of the tool, and a second extension lever for the propping hinged at the end of said first base lever, whereby said second extension lever for the propping presents two propping support teeth, one support teeth at the end and one support teeth close to its articulation to the print base lever.

Figure 41—Call-Outs: Retyped

Call-Out Layouts

There are numerous ways to lay out call-outs. For the sake of easy comparison, we will use the retyped call-out for the various layout examples.

Basic Layout

The basic call-out layout has some variation of the document in the background with the call-out text highlighted and the called out text in a large box partially overlaying the full-page document. Any of these factors—highlight color, use of highlighting at all, call-out placement in relation to the document, etc.—are subject to variation.

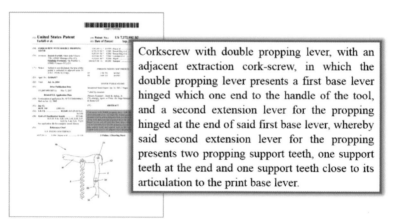

Figure 42—Call-Out Layouts: Basic

Basic Layout with "Pop-Out" Indicator

The basic layout can be supplemented with a "pop-out" indicator. This element shows where the call-out came from and gives it a look as if the call-out is popping out of the original document. Pop-out indicators are typically a solid shape, a shape with a gradient and potentially semi-transparent fill, or lines connecting the call-out location in the full document to the call-out itself.

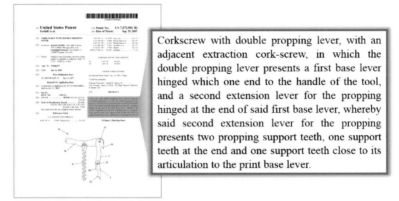

Figure 43—Call-Out Layouts: Pop-Out

Thumbnail Layout

The thumbnail layout has a small image of the full document in the corner without any indication where the call-out came from. In fact, the thumbnail will often be the first page of a multi-page document and may not even contain the text of the call-out, which comes from an interior page. The call-out then takes up most of the available space on the demonstrative. It may or may not overlay the thumbnail.

Corkscrew with double propping lever, with an adjacent extraction cork-screw, in which the double propping lever presents a first base lever hinged which one end to the handle of the tool, and a second extension lever for the propping hinged at the end of said first base lever, whereby said second extension lever for the propping presents two propping support teeth, one support teeth at the end and one support teeth close to its articulation to the print base lever.

Figure 44—Call-Out Layouts: Thumbnail

Call-Out Animations

Trial teams sometimes want to animate call-outs to make it even more evident where precisely the call-out came from. Call-out animations generally animate with two or three steps.

Animated Centered Box Call-Out—Two Step

Step 1: The full document is on the screen with the section where the call-out comes from already indicated.

Step 2: The call-out appears or pops out from the document.

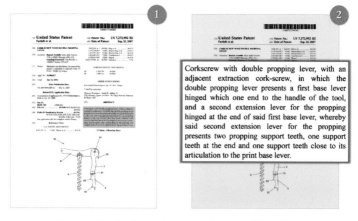

Figure 45—Call-Out Layouts: Animated Two Step

Animated Centered Box Call-Out—Three Step

Step 1: The full document is on the screen.

Step 2: The section where the call-out comes from is indicated on the full document.

Step 3: The call-out appears or pops out from the document.

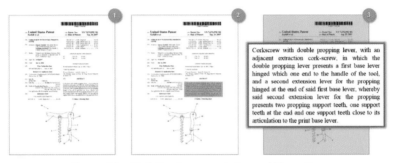

Figure 46—Call-Out Layouts: Animated Three Step

10

Illustrating Data

Data is usually illustrated when you want to show, compare or put in context numbers, totals, etc. Depending on the goal, you may want to show your data in isolation from other data or intersected with it.

Showing Your Data in Isolation

A common example of data shown in isolation is a simple "show your math" calculation, such as for a damages tabulation. As with many of the examples shown previously, the best way to display a chart like the one below may be to introduce each row of data one by one, resulting in the completed chart.

Remediation, Reconstruction & Restatement	$604,000,000
Debt	$524,000,000
Taxes	$210,000,000
Stock Repurchases	$526,000,000
Investor Pilot Program	$295,000,000
Payments to Culpable Parties	+ $75,000,000
Gross Damages	**$2,234,000,000**
Less Recoveries to Date	− $239,000,000
Net Damages	**$1,995,000,000**

Figure 47—Isolated Data: Chart

Another example of showing isolated data is a simple line graph.

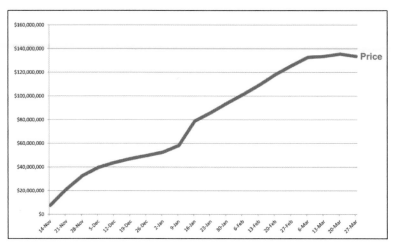

Figure 48—Isolated Data: Graph

Intersecting Your Data

There are times when the interplay between different pieces of information is most relevant to the point being made. Intersection of the relevant data will highlight the information, which could otherwise be hard to see in a cohesive manner. To continue with the line graph in Figure 48, you can overlay information such as relevant periods of time, key dates, or financial data. Following is a relatively straightforward intersecting data graph, which overlays the periods of negotiation and performance, as well as specific key dates.

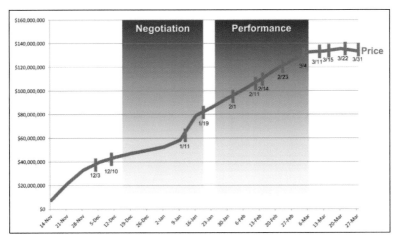

Figure 49—Intersecting Data: Basic Graph

The pieces of information that a trial team can intersect are nearly limitless if there is a common element tying them together. More transaction-specific data can be added: Market data. Securities data. Relevant changes in legislation. Court filings. Court rulings. You name it. The intersections can be highly complex.

But, be forewarned, the more complex the intersection, the more important it is to add data sets one by one, preferably stepping through each data point as you do it (i.e., using a "build"). If you do not build the data step-by-step, you potentially lose the opportunity to make your point. It is too much information to digest all at once.

11

Formatting Shapes and Lines

Shapes

Adjustable Shapes

PowerPoint includes a library of dozens of editable shape objects. The circular arrow at the top of the shape is used to rotate the shape. The yellow boxes are adjustment points that can be dragged to alter the shape's characteristics (i.e., adjusting the curve of a rounded rectangle). And the white boxes are adjustment points that can be dragged to alter the shape's dimensions.

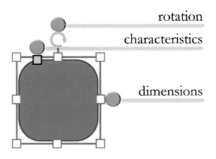

Figure 50—Shapes and Formatting: Adjustable Shapes

Shape Fills

There are four basic shape fills: solid, gradient, pattern, and texture.

Solid. The most basic and most used is the solid color. Its simplicity is often an asset. There are a few things to remember on this point. First, you can create a shape with no fill at all, in which case just the border would be visible as well as everything behind the shape. Second, you can make a shape semi-transparent that, as the description suggests, partially obscures anything behind the shape.

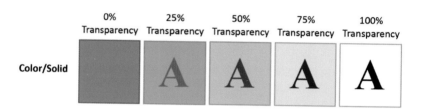

Figure 51—Shapes and Formatting: Solid Color Fill

Gradient. A gradient-filled shape has multiple colors that blend together at determined points. You can select the number of colors, the placement of each color, and the shape the gradient takes as shown in the following example. Gradient-filled shapes are widely used and have a number of useful applications aside from general design considerations as discussed previously with respect to color. An effective use of gradient boxes is for a "pop-out" indicator used with a call-out. The colors used in the gradient pop-out can vary. They can also be the same color but with different transparencies as in Figure 43 in Chapter Nine, *supra*.

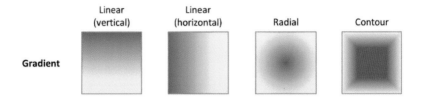

Figure 52—Shapes and Formatting: Gradient Fill

Pattern. The next most common fill is a pattern fill. Although it has limited applications, it can be useful to distinguish one shape from another generally and, as discussed previously, to address any color blindness concerns.

Figure 53—Shapes and Formatting: Pattern Fill

Texture. The least common fill is the texture fill. Occasionally, it is necessary to have a shape filled to look like a particular substance or material. Note that for the texture fill, you can often copy an image into your clipboard and have the option to use that image as the texture, which can be a useful trick if you are trying to recreate a particular background.

Figure 54—Shapes and Formatting: Texture Fill

Shape Effects: Drop Shadows

Drop shadows are used to make the shape or image "pop" off the page, thus emphasizing it. As a result, they should be used sparingly. If overused, then everything is emphasized, which means that nothing is emphasized. Further, the shadow's purpose is to add emphasis but not be a distraction. Accordingly, be cautious before using more perceptible shadows such as floating and perspective. They can look cool, but can detract from your message. It is worth noting that details this subtle are unlikely to be seen when displayed using the most common means, such as a run-of-the-mill projector, even though they may show up on a high-definition computer or external screen.

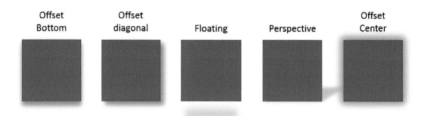

Figure 55—Shapes and Formatting: Shape Effect, Drop Shadows

Shape Effects: Glow

Glow is similar to drop shadows in that it emphasizes the object with the effect. It is useful in making one particular item stand out when there may be a number of similar items, such as an entry on a timeline or a particular data point. But as with drop shadows, don't overdo it in terms of size of the glow and the number of items to which you apply that effect.

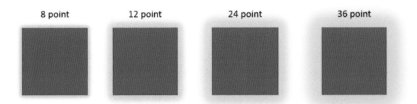

Figure 56—Shapes and Formatting: Shape Effect, Glow

Shape Effects: 3D Effects

Shapes and images can also be rotated in a 3D space. This gives the shapes the look of a physical object that can be useful in recreating generic 3D "illustrations."

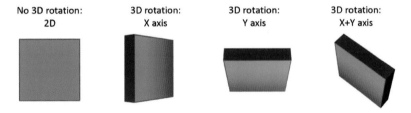

Figure 57—Shapes and Formatting: Shape Effect, 3D Rotation

Shapes and images can also be given depth and bevels. Much like drop shadows and glows, this can give the object emphasis.

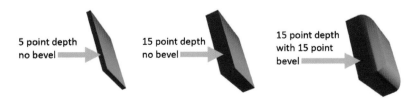

Figure 58—Shapes and Formatting: Shape Effect, 3D Depth, and Bevel

Lines

Different line styles can be used to enhance and complement the color themes and messaging already integrated in the thought process and design of the demonstratives.

Line Styles

Figure 59—Shapes and Formatting: Line Styles

Line Caps

Different line cap types like arrow, ball, and diamond can help emphasize the item at the terminus of the line. Lines with no end cap per se can also be rounded for a softer look or kept square for a more angular appearance.

Figure 60—Shapes and Formatting: Line Caps

12

Illustrations

There are a variety of illustration types used in demonstratives. What to show in an illustration and how to show it all depend on the purpose for the illustration. There are two major factors in graphic illustrations: 2D and 3D Illustrations and Perspective.

2D and 3D Illustrations

2D Illustrations

For the purposes of demonstratives, what makes an illustration 2D or 3D is the software used to create it. This may seem like an arbitrary distinction, especially since it is possible to make a 3D illustration look 2D and a 2D illustration look 3D. But the reason the software matters is that illustrations made with 2D drawing software cannot be rotated in space. Think of it as the digital equivalent to drawing on paper. This means that you cannot change the angle of a 2D illustration without altering the drawing. As a result, you cannot create a 3D animation from a 2D drawing that requires any realistic looking movement in space where the angles and perspectives change even slightly. If your goal is still imagery from one vantage point, then 2D may be best suited for the job.

3D Illustrations

Unlike 2D illustration software, where you create images using lines, shapes, colors, etc., with 3D software, you do not "draw" an image at all. Instead, you create a digital 3D model or series of models, analogous to making sculptures. Creating 3D models and the resulting still images or animation is more time-consuming and expensive than 2D, but is vastly more flexible and can be made to look photo or near-photo realistic because of the nature of 3D models. Once the 3D model is created, it can be rotated or moved in any direction, stills can be created, or the model can be printed with a 3D printer.

Illustration Views

Most still images can be created using 2D or 3D software since the main difference in the two types of software is functional. Either way, it is important to know the different illustration views so that you can communicate precisely about your demonstratives. Following are the different types.

Flat/Bird's-Eye

Flat illustrations (also called "bird's-eye" illustrations) have no indication of 3D space. They are typically a straight-on image of a top, side, or bottom of the object being depicted and made with standard illustration programs. It has no representation of volume or depth, as in the following diagram.

Figure 61—Illustration Views: Flat Diagram

Here is a flat/bird's-eye view illustration.

Figure 62—Illustration Views: Flat Example (2D Illustration)

1-Point Perspective

Unlike a flat drawing, there are multiple ways to represent volume and depth. To understand how to make flat drawings look as if they have depth and volume, you first need to understand what a vanishing point is. Vanishing point is where 2D lines converge on a point off in the distance, giving the illustration a feeling of depth. Use of vanishing points give a 2D image a 3D look.

Using 1-point perspective (which you should think of as 1-*vanishing* point perspective) means that your image has—you guessed it—one vanishing point. Figure 63 shows a box with 1-point perspective.

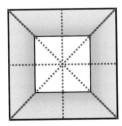

Figure 63—Illustration Views: 1-Point Perspective Diagram (2D Illustration)

The ultimate example of vanishing points generally and 1-point perspective in particular is Leonardo Da Vinci's *The Last Supper*. As shown here, all of the vanishing point lines converge on the same exact point on the horizon in the distance.

Figure 64—Illustration Views: The Ultimate 1-Point Perspective Example, Da Vinci's *The Last Supper*

One-point perspective can have the viewer looking off in the distance from inside a room or a box—such as in the Da Vinci painting. Another way to have 1-point perspective is by having the viewer look from the top, side, or bottom of an object.

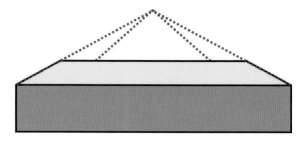

Figure 65—Illustration Views: 1-Point Perspective Diagram with Top View (2D Illustration)

Whether viewed inside or outside of a box, 1-point perspective requires that the vertical X axis and horizontal Y axis be at a right angle and that all lines on the depth Z axis converge on the same point in the distance. Here is a 1-point perspective illustration.

Figure 66—Illustration Views: 1-Point Perspective Example with Top View (2D Illustration)

2-Point Perspective

An image with 2-point perspective has two vanishing points. The result of this is that you can only see two sides of an object, and one of the three axes (X, Y, or Z) must *not* be angled toward or away from the viewer. To understand, look at the next diagram. There are two vanishing points, one off of each side of the box. They are each on one of the horizontal axes. The third axis, the vertical axis in this diagram, is perfectly straight. It does not appear to you, the viewer, to be angled toward or away from you. If it were, you would have a 3-point perspective drawing, discussed in the next section.

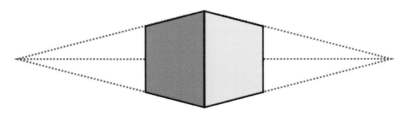

Figure 67—Illustration Views: 2-Point Perspective Diagram (2D Illustration)

Here is an example of a 2-point perspective illustration of the stack of cash shown previously.

Figure 68—Illustration Views: 2-Point Perspective Example (2D Illustration)

3-Point Perspective

As you probably guessed, 3-point perspective has three vanishing points. The result is that all three axes are angled toward or away from the viewer as seen in the next example.

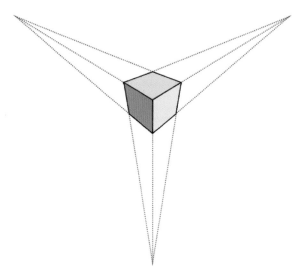

Figure 69—Illustration Views: 3-Point Perspective Diagram

Here is an example of a 3-point perspective illustration.

Figure 70—Illustration Views: 3-Point Perspective Example

Isometric

Isometric drawings are similar to 3-point perspective drawings but with a significant difference. Look at the diagram in Figure 71. It's a nice cube, but something about it doesn't look quite right. The reason is that all of the lines on each axis are parallel. So it implies 3D but has no vanishing points. The lines never converge. So the back of the cube is the exact same size as the front, which is counter to how the brain processes depth. This is not to say that all isometric illustrations are bad or that you should never use them. But if you do, use them sparingly because they will never look quite right to the typical viewer.

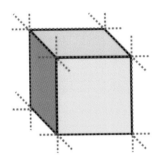

Figure 71—Illustration Views: Isometric Diagram

Here is an example of an isometric illustration.

Figure 72—Illustration Views: Isometric Example (2D Illustration)

Combined Views

Combining multiple illustration views can make a point clearer. This 3D demonstrative on the left shows a car being video-recorded. The image on the right shows the 2D view as seen through the camera. The multiple vantage points make clear what's being recorded and what the recording looks like.

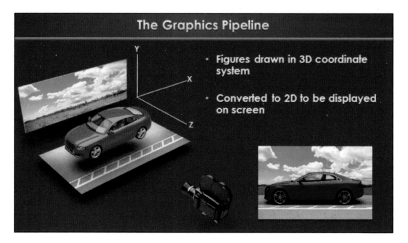

Figure 73—Illustration Views: Combined Views

Illustration Types

Solid/Opaque

Figure 74 is an opaque 2D illustration of the solid exterior of a corkscrew, cork, and wine bottle. Since the illustration is flat, it does not appear to have any depth.

Figure 74—Illustration Types: Solid/Opaque
(2D Illustration: Flat)

Contrast that illustration with Figure 75, a still image of a 3D model of an inhaler. As with almost all 3D model renderings, it has 3-point perspective. The exterior has been rendered as solid and opaque, which is how it would be seen in the "real world."

Figure 75—Illustration Types: Solid/Opaque
(3D Model Still Render:
3-Point Perspective)

Ghosted

Figure 76 is zoomed in on the top of the inhaler with the exterior semi-transparent, typically referred to as "ghosted." This allows you to simultaneously see multiple overlapping layers of the object being depicted. The result is that you can see overlapping interior components and the exterior shell all at the same time. Ghosted 3D images and animations are powerful in that they can allow you to see detail and movement not otherwise visible due to size and/or obstruction.

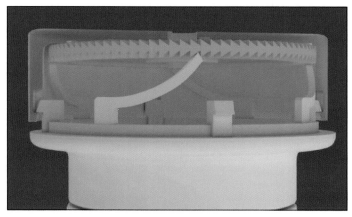

Figure 76—Ilustration Types: Ghosted (3D Model Still Render: 3-Point Perspective)

Cross-Sections

Cross-sections allow you to see one "slice" of the inside of an object as if it has been cut through with a knife. Because of the 2D nature of cross-sections, they are typically flat drawings, although they can have perspective. For simpler mechanisms, cross-sections are an easy way to depict and view interior components.

Figure 77—Illustration Types: Cross-Section (2D Illustration: Flat)

Another way to create cross-sections is to use cross-hatching (criss-cross) fill to indicate the separated or "cut" portions of the object depicted. This is how engineers typically show cross-sections and has advantages when printing in black and white.

Figure 78—Illustration Types:
Cross-Section with Cross-Hatching
(2D Illustration: Flat)

Cut-Aways

Whereas ghosted images allow you to see multiple interior and exterior overlapping layers and cross-sections are isolated to one layer, a cut-away is something of a combination of the two. A cut-away is similar to ghosted because it shows multiple layers at once, yet also similar to a cross-section because the layers it shows are opaque. Cut-aways can be shown in 2D or 3D.

Figure 79—Illustration Types:
Cut-Aways
(2D Illustration:
Isometric)

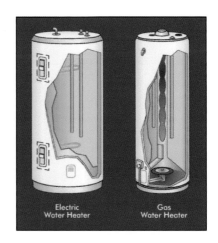

Exploded and Exploding

Exploded views are where the opaque components of an object are all separated out in space so that you can see how they fit together. Exploded views help to show how a mechanism works, how something is constructed, etc. The example below is an exploded view from a medical device patent. It shows how the screws, plates, body, etc., fit together.

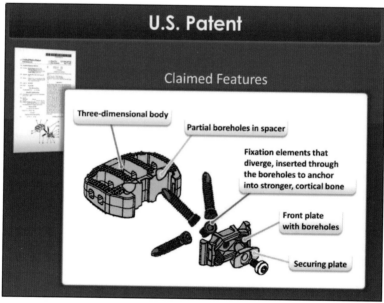

Figure 80—Illustration Types: Exploded View
(3D Illustration: 3-Point Perspective)

Similar to an exploded view is an exploding view. This view is when an object's components are depicted together and are then animated while being removed one-by-one or in groups to show what is inside or underneath. The difference is that the layers or pieces removed do not remain on the screen. They are removed completely. This technique is akin to "showing your work." You start with the entire object and peel away the irrelevant layers or pieces, orienting and focusing the viewer on what matters. In the following animation stills, the apartment building roof and top floors are removed or exploded.

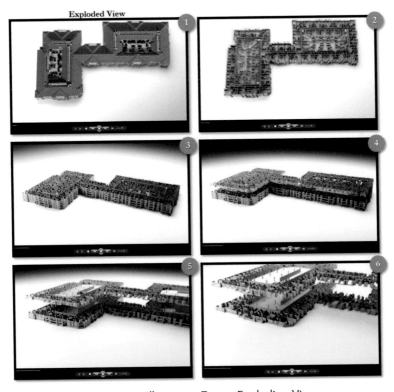

Figure 81—Illustration Types: Exploding View
(3D Animation Still Render: 3-Point Perspective)

After the upper floors are gone, the video then reveals the ground floor units relevant to the case.

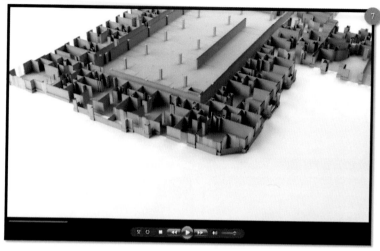

Figure 82—Illustration Types: Exploding View Result
(3D Animation Still Render: 3-Point Perspective)

Specialty Illustrations

Some cases require specialty illustrations. Three notable examples are matters requiring patent figures, construction drawings, and medical illustrations.

Patent Figures

Patents often need technical illustrations in which each component, process, chemical structure, or whatever else is the subject of the patent is labeled. Patent drawings are black and white line drawings and can vary from flat, to perspective, to cross-sections, etc., as the following examples from the same patent demonstrate. As discussed throughout this book, patent figures are often incorporated into demonstratives. In demonstratives, black and white patent figures are often color-coded for emphasis, contrast, comparison, or for directing the viewer to the component being discussed. Here is an example of a flat patent illustration.

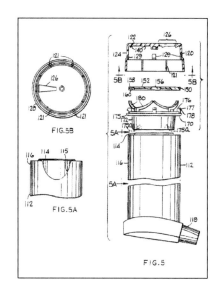

Figure 83—Patent Figure
Illustratrations: Flat
(2D Illustration)

This next example, from the same patent, is an illustration using perspective.

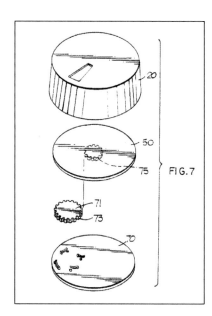

Figure 84—Patent Figure
Illustratrations: Isometric
(2D Illustration, Perspective)

This next example, also from the same patent, shows a cross-section.

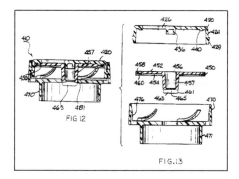

Figure 85—Patent Figure Illustratrations: Cross-Section (2D Illustration, Cross-Hatching)

Construction Drawings

Construction invariably involves illustrations. There are architectural plans, floor plans, elevations, complex scheduling charts, etc. Thus, it is little surprise that construction cases incorporate illustrations and demonstratives. Figure 86 shows the floor plan of a single floor of a building. Each unit is identified with the name of the drywall manufacturer.

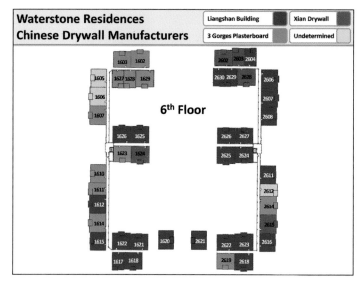

Figure 86—Construction Floor Plan: Bird's-Eye (2D Illustration)

The next illustration is a combination of all six floor plans in an isometric view, making it possible to see the drywall manufacturers by unit as if the exterior of the building were stripped away. This demonstrative was used to create a map of the drywall in the building by manufacturer. This allowed the attorneys to see if there was a pattern on particular floors or in particular sections of the building.

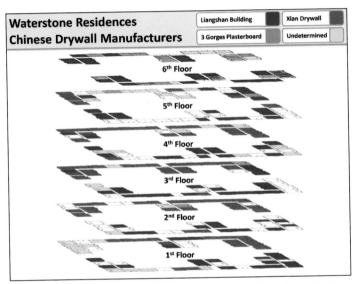

Figure 87—Construction Floor Plan: Isometric (2D Illustration)

3D illustrations and animations also play a big role in large construction cases. If properly sponsored by an expert or fact witness, 3D illustration and animation can effectively show aspects of the building or site that would otherwise be hard or impossible to see.

Figure 88 shows the beginning of a 3D construction animation (and screen shots). The animation was used for a construction defect case where a renovation affected some of the rooms in the building. Below is a bird's-eye view of the digital 3D model of the building.

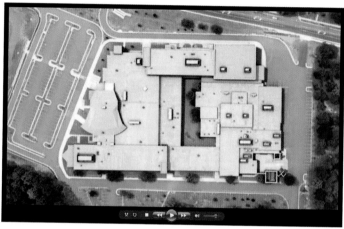

Figure 88—Construction 3D Modeling and Animation: Bird's-Eye

The video then showed a "fly-around" of the building as if the viewer was in a helicopter above, showing the building in 3-point perspective.

Figure 89—Construction 3D Modeling and Animation: 3-Point Perspective

The exterior and much of the interior was then cut away to draw attention to the two rooms relevant to the case, which were ghosted and color-coded blue and green to distinguish them.

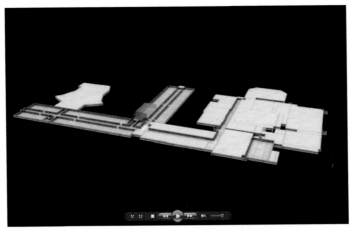

Figure 90—Construction 3D Modeling and Animation:
Ghosted and Cut-Away 3-Point Perspective

The video then showed the construction issues behind the cabinets in the relevant rooms.

Figure 91—Construction 3D Modeling & Animation: Showing the Issue

Medical Illustrations

Medical illustration is its own discipline. Certified medical illustrators (CMIs) are required to have years of rigorous education and training. Medical illustrations can be useful in cases involving anything biomedical, pharmacological, biomechanical, etc., such as patent, tort, and medical malpractice cases. Figure 92 is an example of enterohepatic recirculation, created by a CMI. It is accurate and clear.

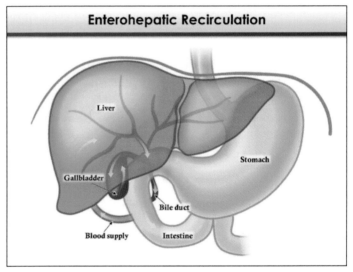

Figure 92—Medical Illustration: Certified Medical Illustrator

For the sake of comparison, an internet search for "enterohepatic recirculation" yields far inferior results—see the screenshot in Figure 93.

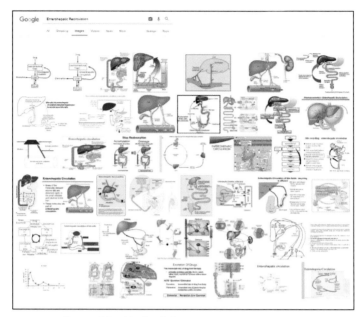

Figure 93—Medical Illustration: Internet Images

Long story short: As with most things in life, you get what you pay for.

13

Tables

Tables are a common tool used in demonstratives and can be an effective way to show data and lists. A basic table has neutral cell borders (row and column lines) and does not emphasize any one piece of data or information.

Basic Table

	1	2	3
First	A1	A2	A3
Second	B1	B2	B3
Third	C1	C2	C3

Figure 94—Tables: Basic

Header Row Emphasis

To make the header more noticeable (or "pop"), you can emphasize it by using a different color in the header row. The color has a much greater impact than just bolding the text in the header row, as is shown in Figure 94.

	1	2	3
First	A1	A2	A3
Second	B1	B2	B3
Third	C1	C2	C3

Figure 95—Tables: Header Row Emphasis

Banded Rows or Columns

Banded rows or columns allow you to more easily distinguish data in different rows or columns. Banding is simply using alternating fill colors, typically muted tones that still make the text easy to read.

	1	2	3
First	A1	A2	A3
Second	B1	B2	B3
Third	C1	C2	C3

Figure 96—Tables: Banded Rows

Cell Borders

Cell borders are also an option when distinguishing rows or columns. As a general rule, if you have banded rows, you will not need cell borders to separate the rows, but cell borders to separate the columns are a good option. The same applies for banded columns; cell borders to separate the columns are not necessary.

	1	2	3
First	A1	A2	A3
Second	B1	B2	B3
Third	C1	C2	C3

Figure 97—Tables: Cell Borders

Ultimately, there is no single right way to design tables. The key, as with all things regarding demonstratives, is that the information most relevant to your case is clear and emphasized.

14

Text Formatting

There are thousands of fonts, but only a few basics you need to know. The caveat with fonts is that preferences are highly personal. In general, there is no right or wrong use of fonts, but there are guidelines you should keep in mind.

Font Types

Serif fonts have small lines that extend off of the tips of the letters, conveniently called serifs! Common serif fonts are Times New Roman, Garamond, and Courier New. As a general rule, serif fonts are the easiest type to read on paper. The serifs help guide your eyes through dense text.

Sans Serif fonts, you guessed it, don't have serifs. Typical sans serif fonts are Helvetica, Arial, and Calibri. Sans serif fonts are the easiest type to read on a screen. The lack of serifs makes the screen less busy, and screen presentations should never be text heavy!

Condensed fonts have skinnier letters. This can be helpful if you are trying to squeeze text into tight spaces, as on a timeline.

Script fonts are—well—script. The rule here is easy, never use them except for wedding invitations.

Here are a few examples of font types.

Serif   Sans serif

Condensed   *Script*

Figure 98—Text Formatting: Font Types

Font Styles

Font styles—**bold**, *italics*, <u>underline</u>, or some combination thereof—are all about emphasis. An unstylized font won't draw your eye as much as an **emphasized** font style. Then again . . . ***if you emphasize everything you end up emphasizing nothing while making the text distracting and hard to read***. Following are a few examples of font styles.

Black   **Bold**   Standard

Italics   <u>Underline</u>

Figure 99—Text Formatting: Font Styles

It is worth pointing out that underlining is the most inferior form of emphasis because it cuts off the bottoms of letters. As you can see in this sentence, the bottoms of the lowercase letters <u>g, j, p, q, and y and of the commas</u> all are cut off. The result is that reading text with underlining requires more brain effort.[1]

---

1. Ruth Anne Robbins, *Painting with Print: Incorporating Concepts of Typographic and Layout Design into the Text of Legal Writing Documents*, J. OF THE ASS'N OF LEGAL WRITING DIRECTORS (2004).

Kerning/Character Spacing

There are a few typography terms related to text that are helpful to know, if for no other reason than to understand the terminology. Kerning—i.e., character spacing—is one of those terms. Standard kerning is what you normally see when you type. This type has standard kerning. You can adjust the kerning to make it tight or loose.

L o o s e   Standard   Tight

Figure 100—Text Formatting: Kerning/Character Spacing

You will almost never need to adjust the kerning. If you are trying to fit text in a tight area, it's better to first try using a condensed font. Or, better yet, reduce the amount of text on the demonstrative.

Leading/Line Spacing

Leading (pronounced "ledding") is the typography term for line spacing. If you make the leading too tight, the words overlap each other and the text is hard to read.

Corkscrew with double propping lever, with an adjacent extraction cork-screw, in which the double propping lever presents a first base lever hinged which one end to the handle of the tool, and a second extension lever for the propping hinged at the end of said first base lever, whereby said second extension lever for the propping presents two propping support teeth, one support teeth at the end and one support teeth close to its articulation to the print base lever.

Figure 101—Text Formatting: Leading/Line Spacing, Too Tight

The problem is further compounded when both the leading and the kerning are too tight.

Corkscrew with double propping lever, with an adjacent extraction cork-screw, in which the double propping lever presents a first base lever hinged which one end to the handle of the tool, and a second extension lever for the propping hinged at the end of said first base lever, whereby said second extension lever for the propping presents two propping support teeth, one support teeth at the end and one support teeth close to its articulation to the print base lever.

Figure 102—Text Formatting: Leading/Line Spacing and Kerning, Too Tight

If need be for reasons of limited real estate on the page or screen, it is okay to tighten up the leading, provided you keep an eye on the potential overlap issue. The following example has condensed leading with sufficiently distinct lines of text.

Corkscrew with double propping lever, with an adjacent extraction cork-screw, in which the double propping lever presents a first base lever hinged which one end to the handle of the tool, and a second extension lever for the propping hinged at the end of said first base lever, whereby said second extension lever for the propping presents two propping support teeth, one support teeth at the end and one support teeth close to its articulation to the print base lever.

Figure 103—Text Formatting: Leading/Line Spacing, Tight

Type Effects

As seen in the examples that follow, most programs allow you to add effects to text similar to effects that can be applied to shapes. Unless you have a specific design reason for using these effects, it is better to avoid using them as they are usually distracting and tend not to help move the needle toward winning your case.

One exception is the use of drop shadows and glow effects. Drop shadows make the text look like it is lifted off the page—i.e., they make it "pop." This is good for emphasizing a particular piece of information and also for contrasting the text from the background. But drop shadows used on dark font colors look muddy and should be avoided. The "light" that causes the drop shadow can come from any direction, including directly overhead, casting the shadow around all the edges of the text. That is essentially the same thing as a glow. Drop shadows default to gray but can be adjusted to other colors. Glows have no set default color.

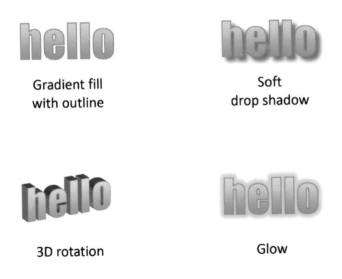

Gradient fill
with outline

Soft
drop shadow

3D rotation

Glow

Figure 104—Text Formatting: Type Effects

Font and Background Colors

In choosing font and background colors, your first job is to make sure that the text is easy to read. Once you have passed that hurdle, you can explore options for color coding to, or color contrasting from, other items on the demonstrative to reinforce messaging. As in Figure 105 on the left, a few things to avoid are drop shadows on dark type, overly contrasting bright color fonts on dark backgrounds, and light color fonts on light backgrounds.

Instead, follow the general guidelines in Figure 105 on the right. If you want to use a dark background, in general use white or yellow color font. If you want to use a light color background, use a dark color font, such as black, dark red, or blue.

Figure 105—Text Formatting:
Guidelines for Easy to Read Font and Background Colors

Capitalization

Some lawyers like to use ALL CAPS for titles or text. Not only is it considered "shouting" in the age of text messaging, it also has distinct drawbacks for demonstratives. The different segments of upper- and lowercase letters make them distinct from each other and, thus, easy to read. All caps letters have uniform height, making them less distinct and harder to read. All caps letters also take up more space.

The result is that sentence case is the easiest to read, SMALL CAPS ARE HARDER TO READ, AND ALL CAPS ARE THE HARDEST. Let us show you why.

Sentence Case:	Comparing different capitalizations
SMALL CAPS:	COMPARING DIFFERENT CAPITALIZATIONS
ALL CAPS:	COMPARING DIFFERENT CAPITALIZATIONS

Figure 106—Capitalization Comparison: Text

To make it easier to see the letter differentiation, below is an image of the blocks of text in the prior figure. The gray bars show the common height of the text, and the red boxes are where particular letters rise above or below.

Figure 107—Capitalization Comparison: Shape

Sentence case has variety above and below. Small caps have no extensions below and fewer above. All caps have no extensions at all. As you can see, the further you move away from sentence case, the less letter differential you have.

Another type of capitalization worth noting is capitalizing each work, often called "Heading Case." Capitalizing Each Word Is A Little Harder To Read Than Sentence Case But Is Sometimes Reserved For Titles. It would look like this in our comparison.

Cap Each Word: Comparing Different Capitalizations

Figure 108—Capitalize Each Word: Text

Capitalizing each word is a bit of an outlier regarding the quantity of letter height differentiation. It has more up segments than sentence case, but it's still harder to read because the larger capital letter at the start of each word breaks up the flow of the text. For comparison's sake, here is the text block version.

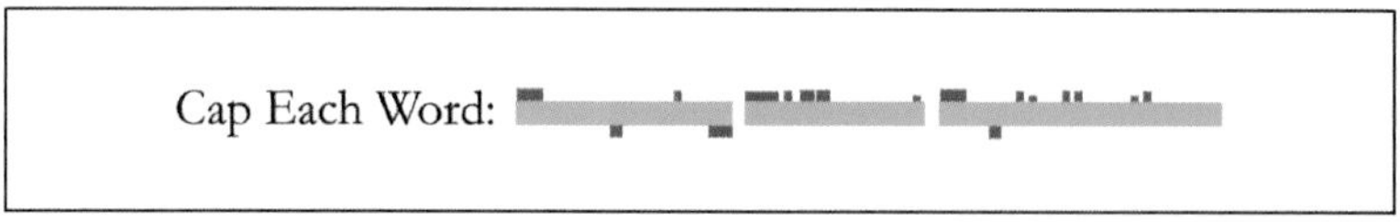

Cap Each Word:

Figure 109—Capitalize Each Word: Shape

Heading case can also be distracting because there are different schools of thought regarding which words should be capitalized and which words should not (primarily, articles and prepositions having fewer than a certain number of letters).

Ultimately, almost all text we read is sentence case; we have trained ourselves as a society to read that way, just as this book is written. If you want to have your audience spend less time deciphering your text and more time focusing on your point, then limit or avoid use of all caps and its variants.

Bullet Lists

Like them or hate them, bullet lists are a staple of demonstratives. They do serve a utilitarian purpose. To make them effective, limit the number of bullets and the amount of text. Use as few words as possible and avoid using bullet points as a crutch so the lawyer or witness remembers what to say. (*See* section titled "Overall Design" in Chapter 8.) It almost always comes across as rehearsed, or worse, that the witness is just saying what the lawyer wanted to say. One strategy that helps the lawyer, but not the witness, is to put all of your bullets in the "notes" section of your slides. (*See* section titled "Witnesses" in Chapter 7.)

The typical bullet list starting point would be like the next example. There is nothing wrong with the example, but there is nothing right about it either.

Figure 110—Bullet Lists: Before

There are a number of basic steps you can take to liven it up and make it more impactful.

Step 1: Break Up the Title

In the example, we have delineated the headline, "Sports Properties" and the subheading, "Dealing with Licensees."

Figure 111—Bullet Lists: Breaking Up the Title

You can also add relevant visual elements to make the demonstrative more engaging.

Figure 112—Bullet Lists: Adding Visual Elements

Step 2: Remove All Redundant Language

In our example, we have removed the repeating words "avoid discussing" and emphasized them above the bullet list.

Figure 113—Bullet Lists: Removing Redundant Language

Step 3: Reformat and Separate the Concluding Bullet

The entire point of the example is that Sports Properties doesn't control competition. By making it stand out, the message is emphasized.

Figure 114—Bullet Lists:
Reformatting and Separating the Concluding Bullet

15

Timelines

Along with document call-outs and bullet lists, timelines are some of the most common demonstratives. The single most important thing to remember is that a well created timeline is more than a mere listing of events. The content and design must show why the events are important. As discussed earlier, remember that demonstratives must mesh G➡S➡V Analysis, Know the User, Lightning Speed Principle, and Differential Emphasis (*see* Chapter 2, *supra*).

Timelines come in all shapes, sizes, and formats, all with different looks, advantages, and disadvantages. We'll start with basic timelines and work our way up.

Stick and Flag Timeline

A standard stick and flag is your "base model" timeline. It shows events but does not make a point. All information is treated equally and, as such, is barely more than a list of events formatted horizontally. This example is not an advocacy graphic.

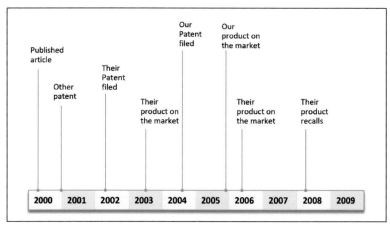

Figure 115—Timelines: Standard Stick and Flag,
Not an Advocacy Graphic

Just because the basic stick and flag timeline doesn't move the needle on your case does not mean it has no merit. There are a number of enhancements you can make that can make your point persuasive. One enhancement you can make is adding icons and color coding to differentiate entries as in Figure 116. All of a sudden, a story starts to take shape with these few enhancements. The icons make it easy to distinguish the patents from the published article. Plus, the color coding distinguishes which events relate to each patent. Then, since the icons are color coded, the opposing party's patent is keyed to events related to their product.

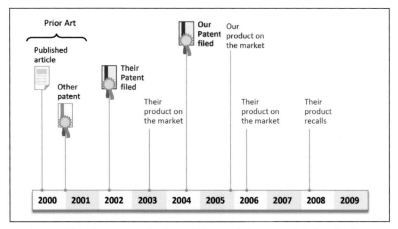

Figure 116—Timelines: Stick and Flag with Icons and Color Coding

There are other options as well. One is to group events by color or with brackets. In Figure 117, the grouping visually links specific events. This grouping changes the timeline from having many small pieces of data that the viewer needs to integrate to only a few chunks of data. Now it is even easier to distinguish the prior art from the events related to the patents at issue in the case.

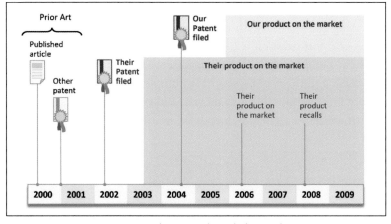

Figure 117—Timelines: Stick and Flag with Icons,
Color Coding, and Grouped Ranges

You can take the timeline further by adding a layer of relevant intersecting data on top of the timeline. In Figure 118, the sales data added on top of the relevant market events help to further paint the picture of the fortunes and misfortunes of the two patented products.

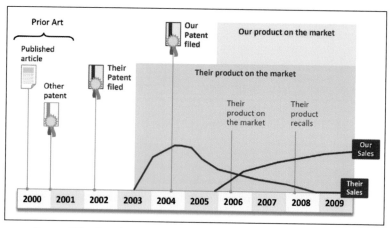

Figure 118—Timelines: Stick and Flag with Icons, Color Coding, Grouped Ranges, and Overlaid Data

A word of caution is warranted at this point. The more data, layers, and visual information you add to a demonstrative, the more you risk confusing the viewer. With timelines that have more than just a few pieces of information, it is highly advisable to add each event one by one in a "build" format. If you are going to add intersecting layers on top, don't add them until you have completely introduced the prior layer of information. If you start at the end with the fully built and layered timeline, you will have lost the viewer from the very beginning.

Hyperlinked Timeline

One operational variant on the timeline is to create hyperlinks in the timeline instead of either having it fully built at the outset or building in a predetermined sequence. This can be helpful if there is a lot of data that cannot all be shown on the face of the timeline or if you would like to have relevant document call-outs appear and disappear as needed. This can be particularly useful for cross-examination when there is no set order of the testimony and jumping around may be required.

Here is an example hyperlinked timeline. All of the dates along the price graph are hyperlinked to key events.

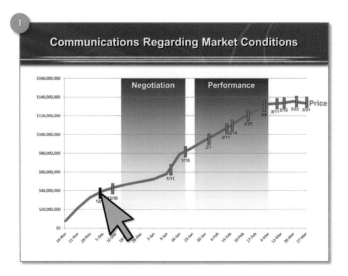

Figure 119—Timelines: Hyperlinked, Selecting the Link

Once you click on the link, the relevant information appears.

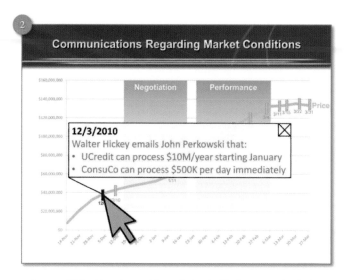

Figure 120—Timelines: Hyperlinked, Clicking on the Link

Close out the box to clear the hyperlinked information.

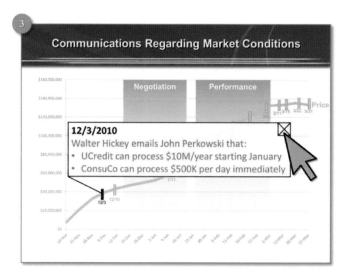

Figure 121—Timelines: Hyperlinked, Closing Out the Box

This brings you back to the timeline.

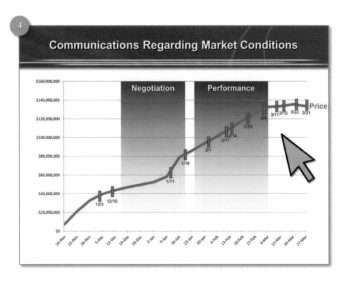

Figure 122—Timelines: Hyperlinked, Back to the Timeline

Banded Timeline

Banded timelines can be used to show frequency or timing of particular kinds of reoccurring events. Each band is a category of event such as a call, email, meeting, text message, etc. Icons can be used to represent when those events happened in relation to each other. In Figure 123, the bands for emails, calls, and memos show the dates and frequencies of these modes of communication at a glance.

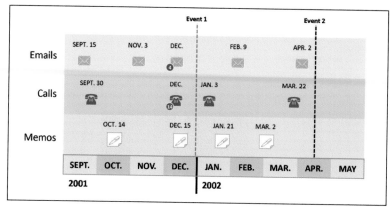

Figure 123—Timelines: Banded

Calendar Timeline

Another way to show repeating events is to use a calendar timeline. It is similar to a banded timeline in the use of icons to represent events on particular days, but it replaces the banding with the calendar grid. This is particularly effective for shorter periods of time such as a few months, although it can be accomplished over a longer span provided there are only a few event types, such as emails and calls.

DECEMBER 1994

SUNDAY	MONDAY	TUESDAY	WEDNESDAY	THURSDAY	FRIDAY	SATURDAY
				1	2	3
4	5	6	7	8	9	10
11	12	13	14	15	16	17
18	19	20	21	22	23	24
25	26	27	28	29	30	31

Figure 124—Timelines: Calendar

16

Inspiration Index

While the preceeding chapters have many examples of different types of demonstratives for a variety of uses, in this Inspiration Index we have categorized those examples by type and added many more. Here you can look for different ideas, concepts, layouts, and the like. Organized by type of demonstrative (noting that some demonstratives incorporate more than one type and accordingly are included in multiple sections), we have included this Inspiration Index as a springboard to help you develop the most persuasive and effective demonstratives to best fit your needs.

Bullet Lists, Charts, and Tables

Figure 125—Inspiration Index: Bullet Lists, Charts, and Tables

Figure 126—Inspiration Index: Bullet Lists, Charts, and Tables

Remediation, Reconstruction & Restatement	$604,000,000
Debt	$524,000,000
Taxes	$210,000,000
Stock Repurchases	$526,000,000
Investor Pilot Program	$295,000,000
Payments to Culpable Parties	+ $75,000,000
Gross Damages	**$2,234,000,000**
Less Recoveries to Date	− $239,000,000
Net Damages	**$1,995,000,000**

Figure 127—Inspiration Index: Bullet Lists, Charts, and Tables

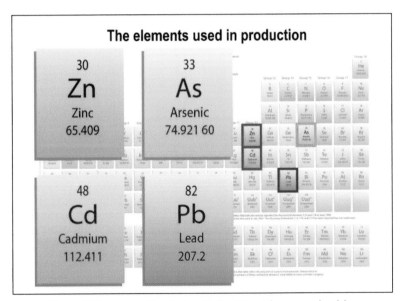

Figure 128—Inspiration Index: Bullet Lists, Charts, and Tables

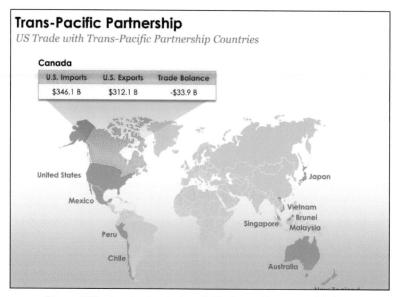

Figure 129—Inspiration Index: Bullet Lists, Charts, and Tables

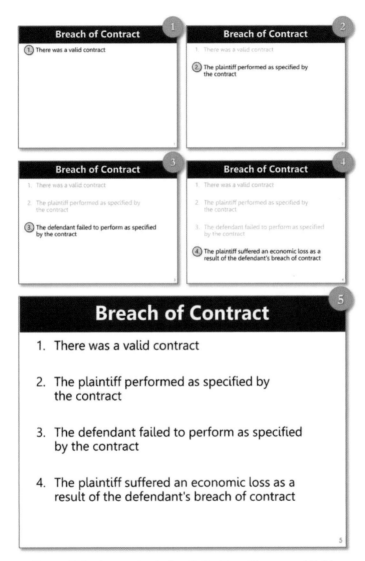

Figure 130—Inspiration Index: Bullet Lists, Charts, and Tables

Methods of Analysis

Blakely

1. Review of redacted and abridged case file
2. Compare with county data

Standard Analysis Method

1. Review full case files
2. Compare with statewide or national data
3. Weight analysis for demographic variances

6

Figure 131—Inspiration Index: Bullet Lists, Charts, and Tables

Mr. Hunter's Flawed Findings

Number of Impacted Findings

1	Breach of Law and Policy	53
2	Conflict of Interest and Side Payments	189
3	Improperly Obtained Information	279
	Total Findings	521

Figure 132—Inspiration Index: Bullet Lists, Charts, and Tables

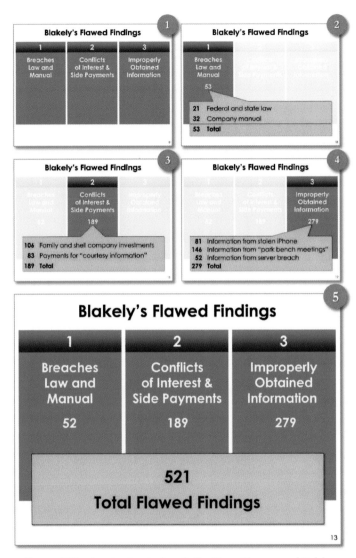

Figure 133—Inspiration Index: Bullet Lists, Charts, and Tables

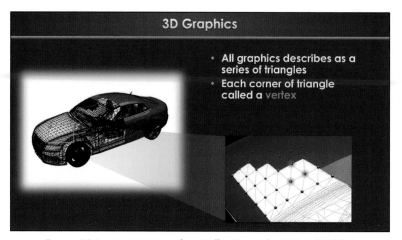

Figure 134—Inspiration Index: Bullet Lists, Charts, and Tables

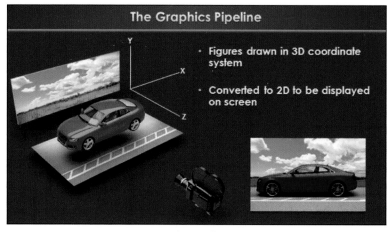

Figure 135—Inspiration Index: Bullet Lists, Charts, and Tables

Comparisons

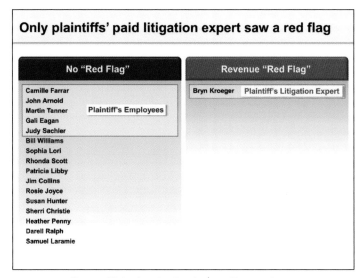

Figure 136—Inspiration Index: Comparisons

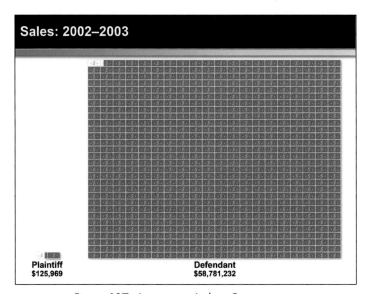

Figure 137—Inspiration Index: Comparisons

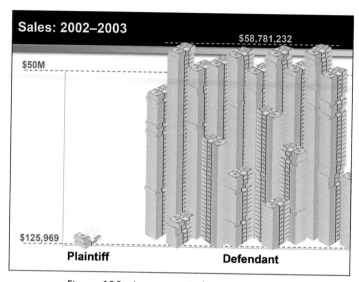

Figure 138—Inspiration Index: Comparisons

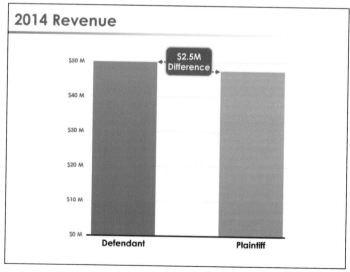

Figure 139—Inspiration Index: Comparisons

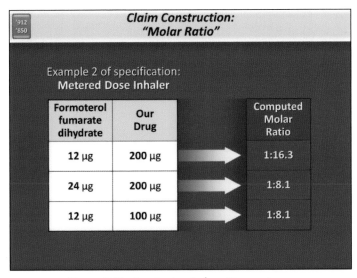

Figure 140—Inspiration Index: Comparisons

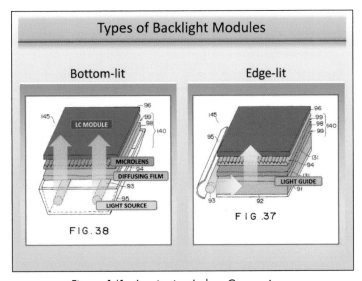

Figure 141—Inspiration Index: Comparisons

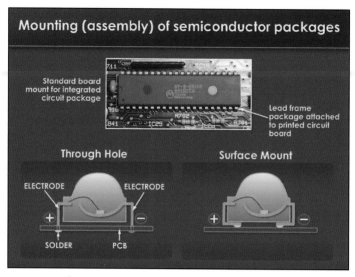

Figure 142—Inspiration Index: Comparisons

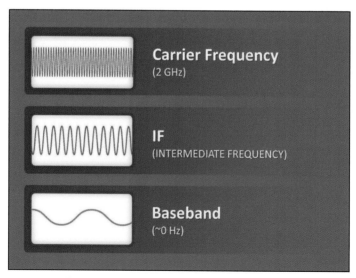

Figure 143—Inspiration Index: Comparisons

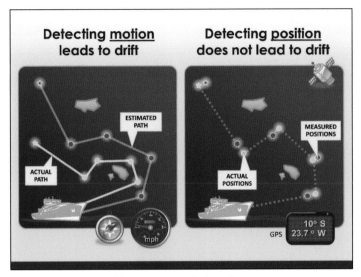

Figure 144—Inspiration Index: Comparisons

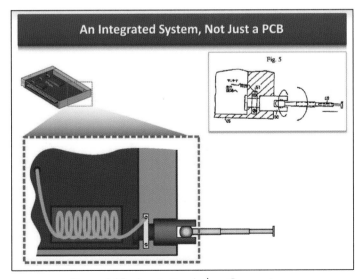

Figure 145—Inspiration Index: Comparisons

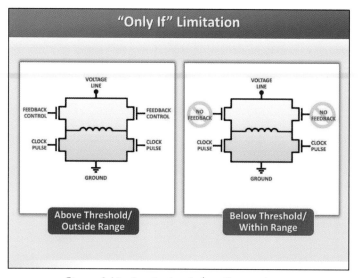

Figure 146—Inspiration Index: Comparisons

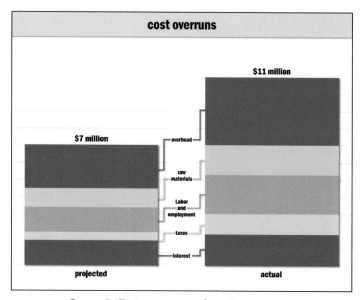

Figure 147—Inspiration Index: Comparisons

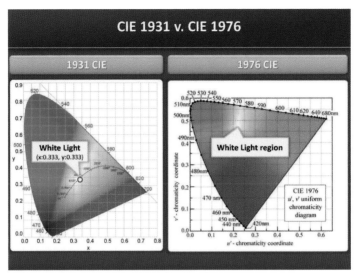

Figure 148—Inspiration Index: Comparisons

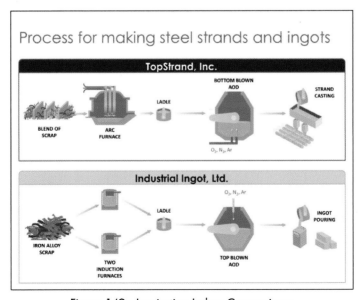

Figure 149—Inspiration Index: Comparisons

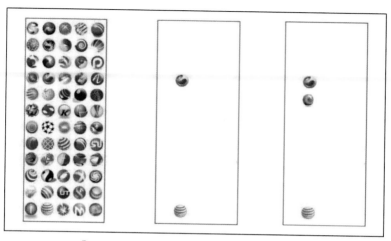

Figure 150—Inspiration Index: Comparisons

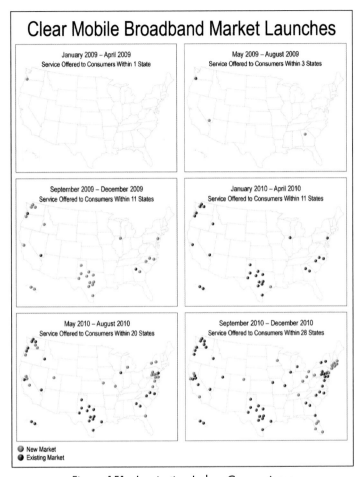

Figure 151—Inspiration Index: Comparisons

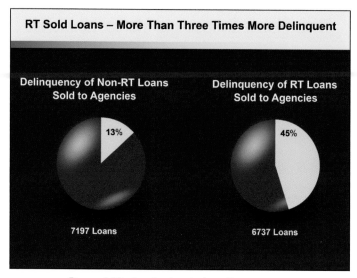

Figure 152—Inspiration Index: Comparisons

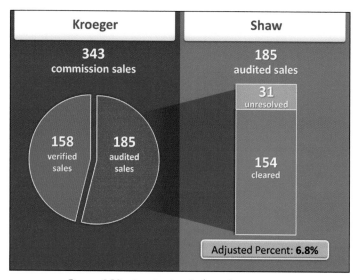

Figure 153—Inspiration Index: Comparisons

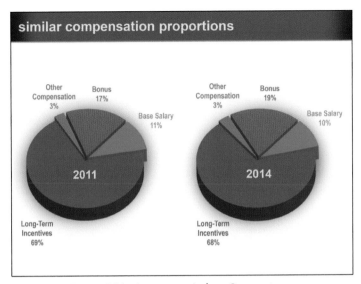

Figure 154—Inspiration Index: Comparisons

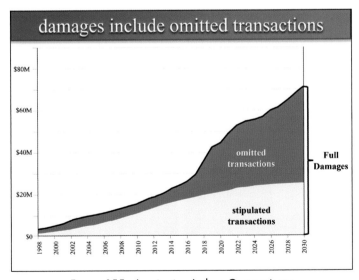

Figure 155—Inspiration Index: Comparisons

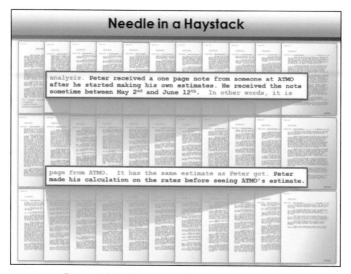

Figure 156—Inspiration Index: Comparisons

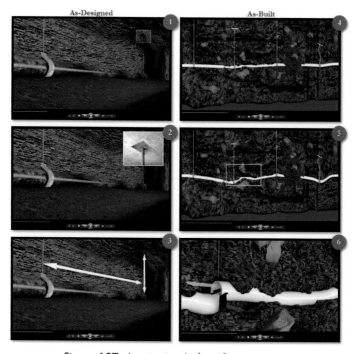

Figure 157—Inspiration Index: Comparisons

Data Charts

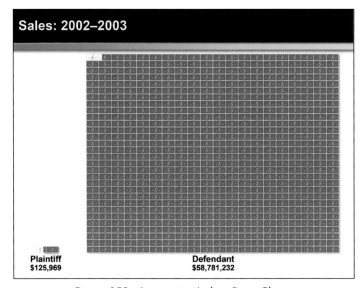

Figure 158—Inspiration Index: Data Charts

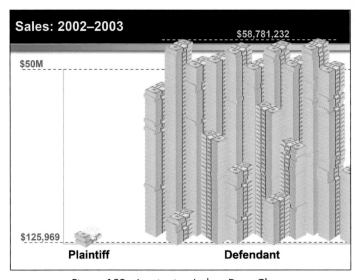

Figure 159—Inspiration Index: Data Charts

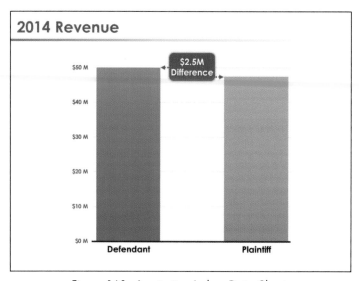

Figure 160—Inspiration Index: Data Charts

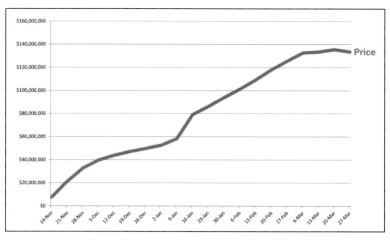

Figure 161—Inspiration Index: Data Charts

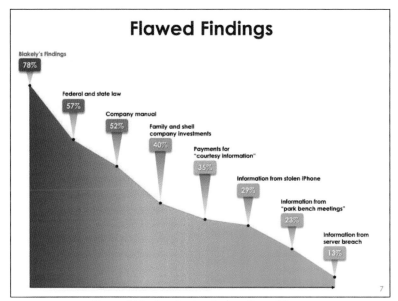

Figure 162—Inspiration Index: Data Charts

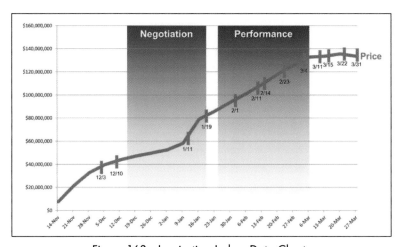

Figure 163—Inspiration Index: Data Charts

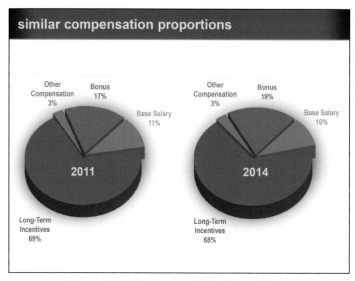

Figure 164—Inspiration Index: Data Charts

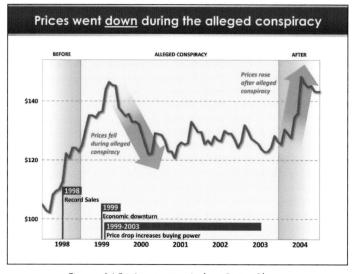

Figure 165—Inspiration Index: Data Charts

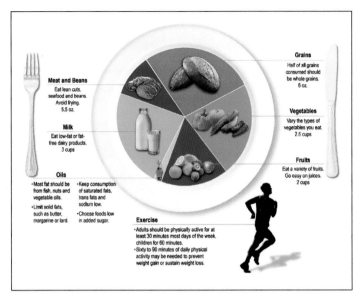

Figure 166—Inspiration Index: Data Charts

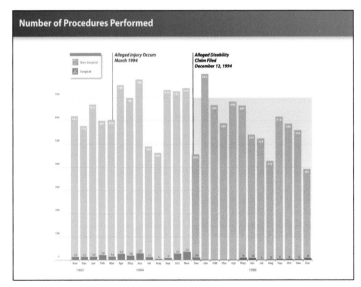

Figure 167—Inspiration Index: Data Charts

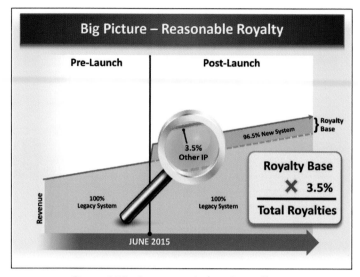

Figure 168—Inspiration Index: Data Charts

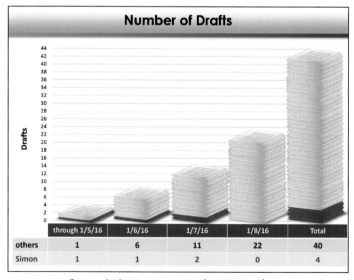

Figure 169—Inspiration Index: Data Charts

Figure 170—Inspiration Index: Data Charts

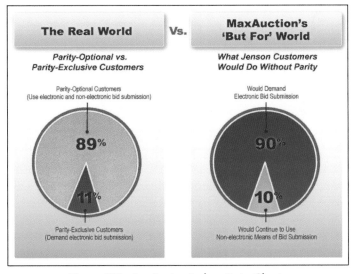

Figure 171—Inspiration Index: Data Charts

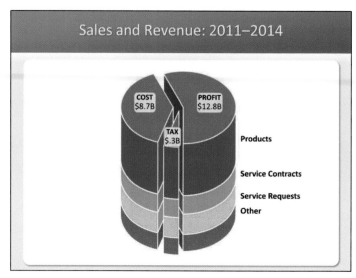

Figure 172—Inspiration Index: Data Charts

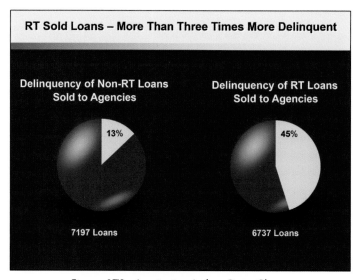

Figure 173—Inspiration Index: Data Charts

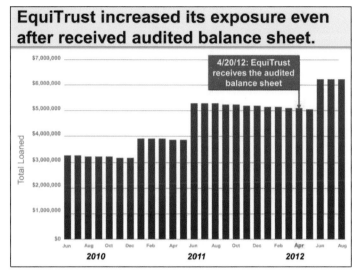

Figure 174—Inspiration Index: Data Charts

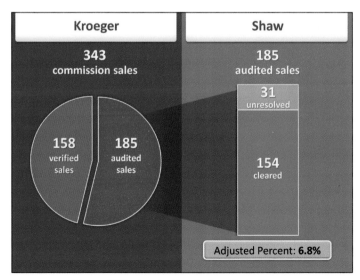

Figure 175—Inspiration Index: Data Charts

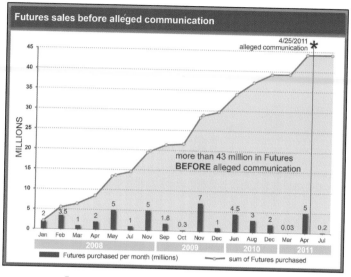

Figure 176—Inspiration Index: Data Charts

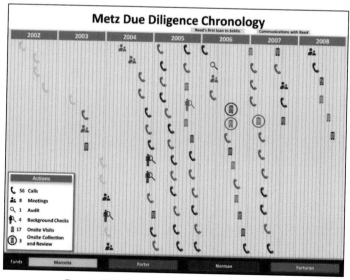

Figure 177—Inspiration Index: Data Charts

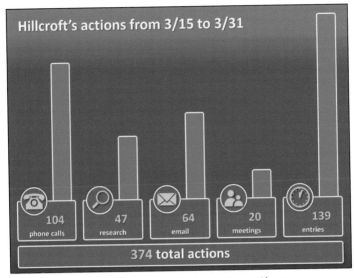

Figure 178—Inspiration Index: Data Charts

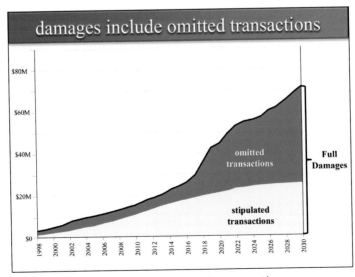

Figure 179—Inspiration Index: Data Charts

Figure 180—Inspiration Index: Data Charts

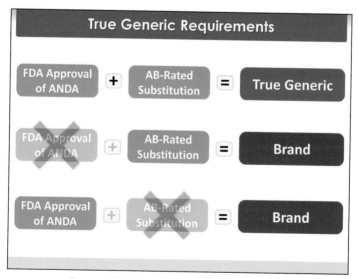

Figure 181—Inspiration Index: Data Charts

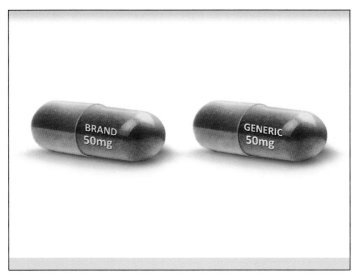

Figure 182—Inspiration Index: Data Charts

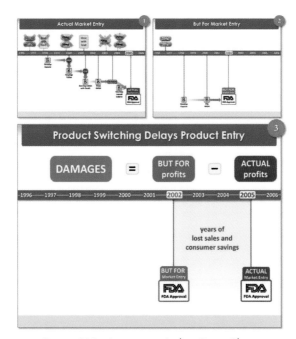

Figure 183—Inspiration Index: Data Charts

Documents and Call-Outs

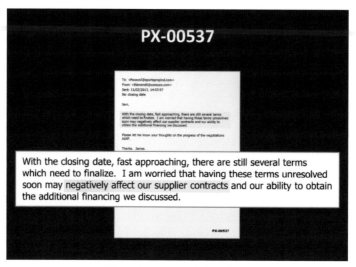

Figure 184—Inspiration Index: Documents

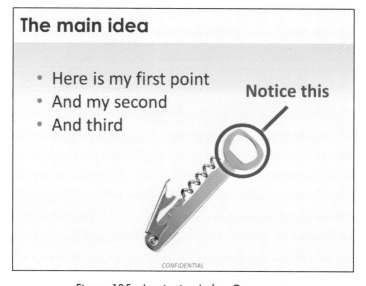

Figure 185—Inspiration Index: Documents

'188 Patent, Fig. 1

a helicoidal body **(6)**

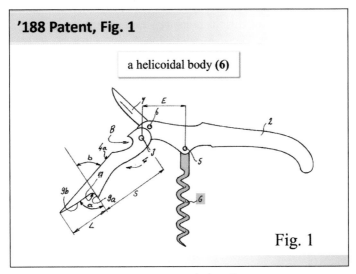

Fig. 1

Figure 186—Inspiration Index: Documents

Corkscrew with double propping lever, with an adjacent extraction cork-screw, in which the double propping lever presents a first base lever hinged which one end to the handle of the tool, and a second extension lever for the propping hinged at the end of said first base lever, whereby said second extension lever for the propping presents two propping support teeth, one support teeth at the end and one support teeth close to its articulation to the print base lever.

Figure 187—Inspiration Index: Documents

Corkscrew with double propping lever, with an adjacent extraction cork-screw, in which the double propping lever presents a first base lever hinged which one end to the handle of the tool, and a second extension lever for the propping hinged at the end of said first base lever, whereby said second extension lever for the propping presents two propping support teeth, one support teeth at the end and one support teeth close to its articulation to the print base lever.

Figure 188—Inspiration Index: Documents

Corkscrew with double propping lever, with an adjacent extraction cork-screw, in which the double propping lever presents a first base lever hinged which one end to the handle of the tool, and a second extension lever for the propping hinged at the end of said first base lever, whereby said second extension lever for the propping presents two propping support teeth, one support teeth at the end and one support teeth close to its articulation to the print base lever.

Figure 189—Inspiration Index: Documents

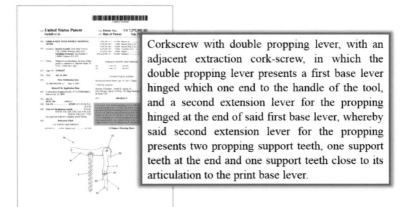

Corkscrew with double propping lever, with an adjacent extraction cork-screw, in which the double propping lever presents a first base lever hinged which one end to the handle of the tool, and a second extension lever for the propping hinged at the end of said first base lever, whereby said second extension lever for the propping presents two propping support teeth, one support teeth at the end and one support teeth close to its articulation to the print base lever.

Figure 190—Inspiration Index: Documents

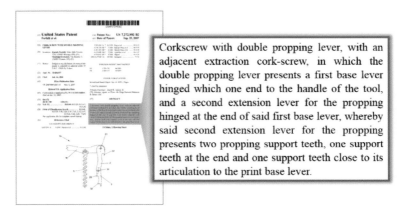

Corkscrew with double propping lever, with an adjacent extraction cork-screw, in which the double propping lever presents a first base lever hinged which one end to the handle of the tool, and a second extension lever for the propping hinged at the end of said first base lever, whereby said second extension lever for the propping presents two propping support teeth, one support teeth at the end and one support teeth close to its articulation to the print base lever.

Figure 191—Inspiration Index: Documents

Corkscrew with double propping lever, with an adjacent extraction cork-screw, in which the double propping lever presents a first base lever hinged which one end to the handle of the tool, and a second extension lever for the propping hinged at the end of said first base lever, whereby said second extension lever for the propping presents two propping support teeth, one support teeth at the end and one support teeth close to its articulation to the print base lever.

Figure 192—Inspiration Index: Documents

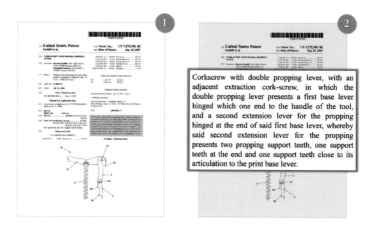

Figure 193—Inspiration Index: Documents

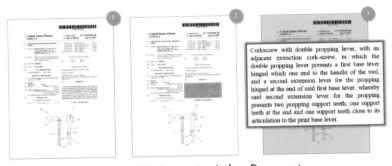

Corkscrew with double propping lever, with an adjacent extraction cork-screw, in which the double propping lever presents a first base lever hinged which one end to the handle of the tool, and a second extension lever for the propping hinged at the end of said first base lever, whereby said second extension lever for the propping presents two propping support teeth, one support teeth at the end and one support teeth close to its articulation to the print base lever.

Figure 194—Inspiration Index: Documents

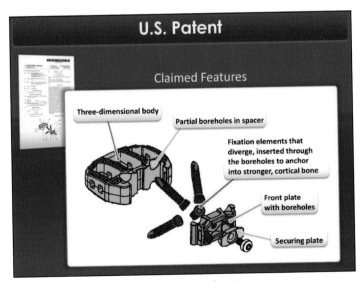

Figure 195—Inspiration Index: Documents

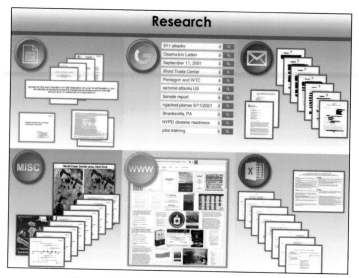

Figure 196—Inspiration Index: Documents

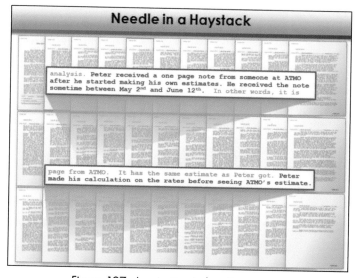

Figure 197—Inspiration Index: Documents

Figure 198—Inspiration Index: Documents

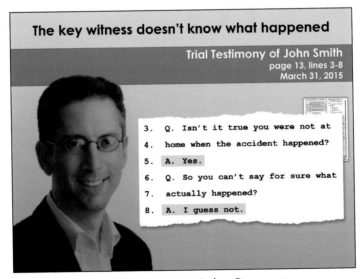

Figure 199—Inspiration Index: Documents

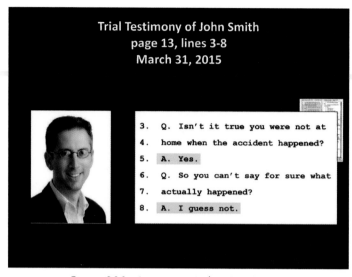

Figure 200—Inspiration Index: Documents

Medical History					
2010	**2011**		**2012**	**2013**	
6/11/2010	**3/22/2011**	**7/4/2011**	**3/11/2012**	**8/18/2013**	**9/9/2013**
Arrhythmia initially diagnosed	Prior claim: shoulder strain	Prior claim: knee strain	Shoulder & neck pain starts	ER visit, chronic neck & shoulder pain	Dr Betz, shoulder & neck pain treatment

Deposition Exhibit 35

Figure 201—Inspiration Index: Documents

Sequenced Map with Call-Outs and Icons

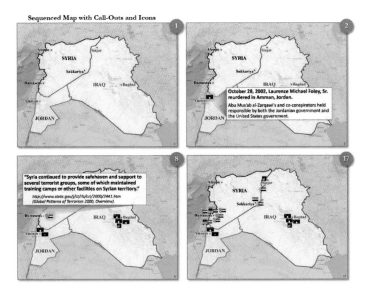

Figure 202—Inspiration Index: Documents

Flow Charts and Processes

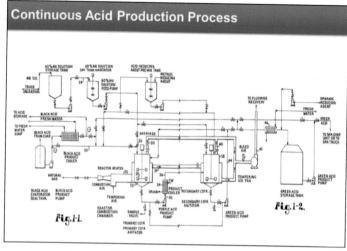

Figure 203—Inspiration Index: Flow Charts

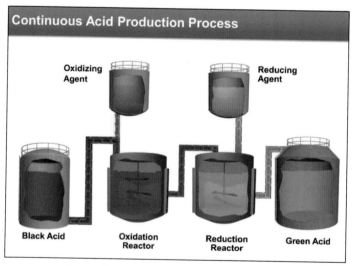

Figure 204—Inspiration Index: Flow Charts

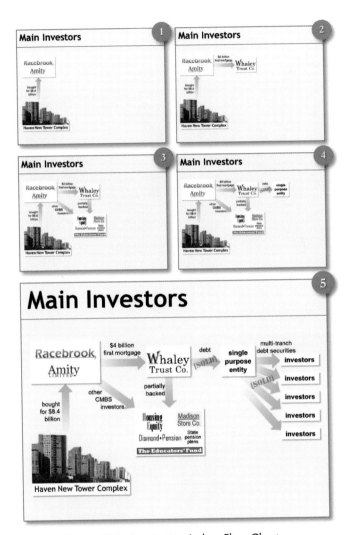

Figure 205—Inspiration Index: Flow Charts

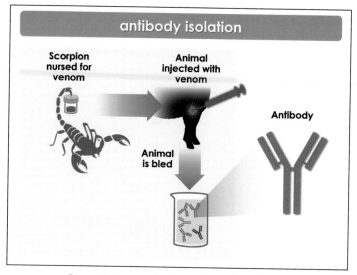

Figure 206—Inspiration Index: Flow Charts

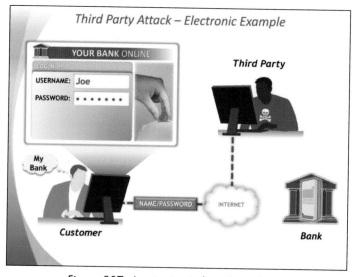

Figure 207—Inspiration Index: Flow Charts

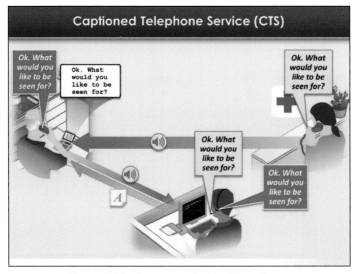

Figure 208—Inspiration Index: Flow Charts

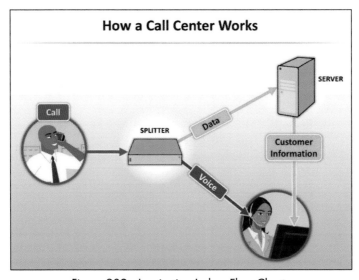

Figure 209—Inspiration Index: Flow Charts

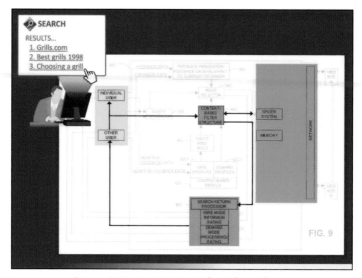

Figure 210—Inspiration Index: Flow Charts

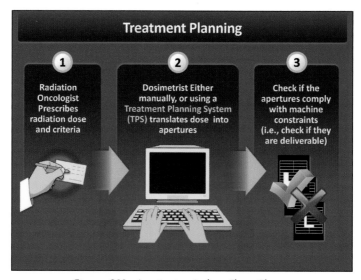

Figure 211—Inspiration Index: Flow Charts

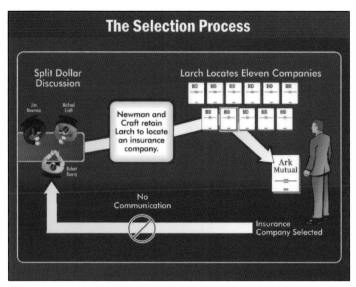

Figure 212—Inspiration Index: Flow Charts

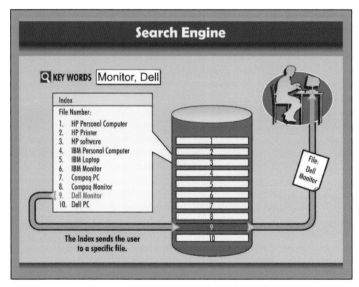

Figure 213—Inspiration Index: Flow Charts

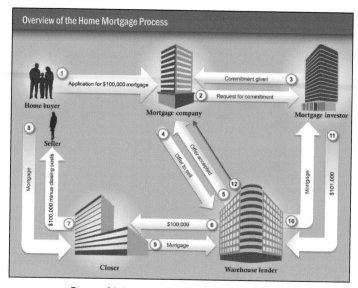

Figure 214—Inspiration Index: Flow Charts

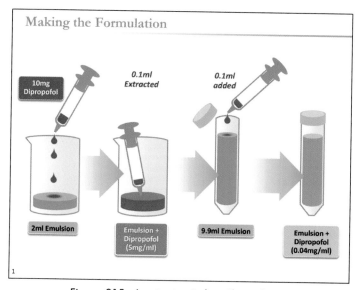

Figure 215—Inspiration Index: Flow Charts

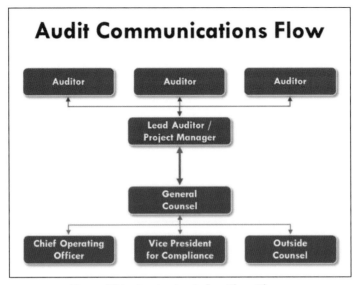

Figure 216—Inspiration Index: Flow Charts

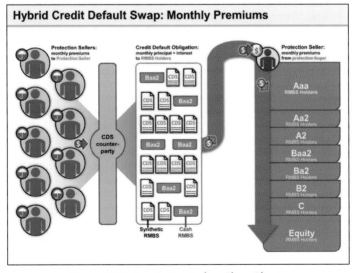

Figure 217—Inspiration Index: Flow Charts

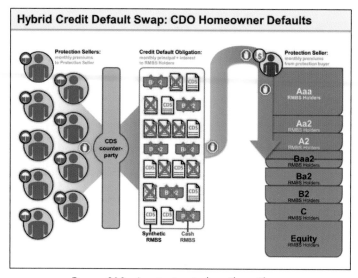

Figure 218—Inspiration Index: Flow Charts

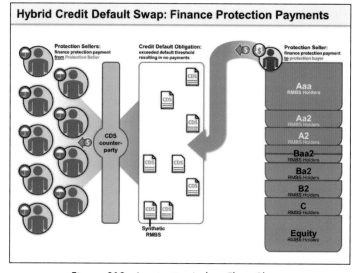

Figure 219—Inspiration Index: Flow Charts

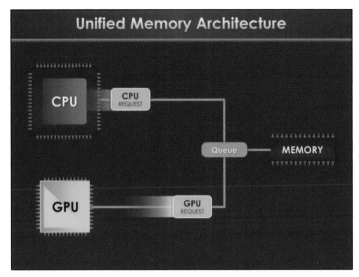

Figure 220—Inspiration Index: Flow Charts

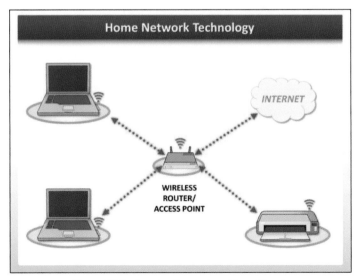

Figure 221—Inspiration Index: Flow Charts

Maps

Figure 222—Inspiration Index: Maps

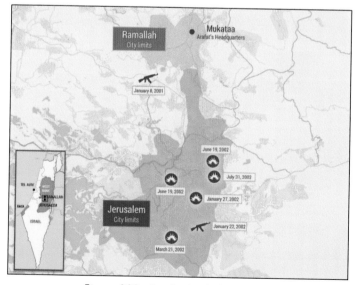

Figure 223—Inspiration Index: Maps

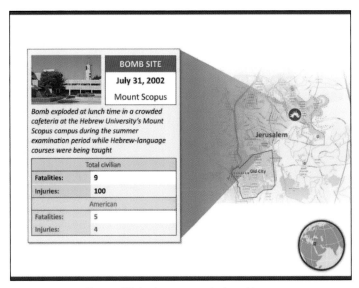

Figure 224—Inspiration Index: Maps

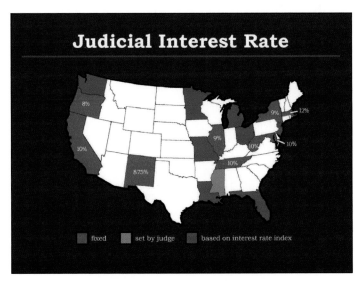

Figure 225—Inspiration Index: Maps

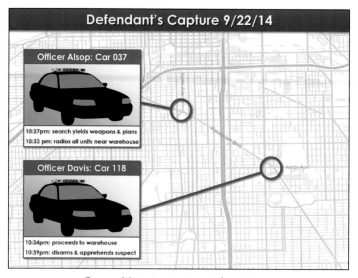

Figure 226—Inspiration Index: Maps

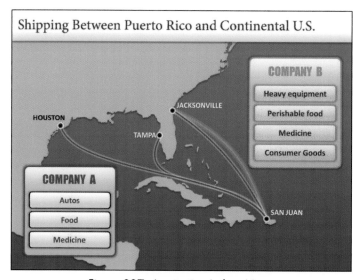

Figure 227—Inspiration Index: Maps

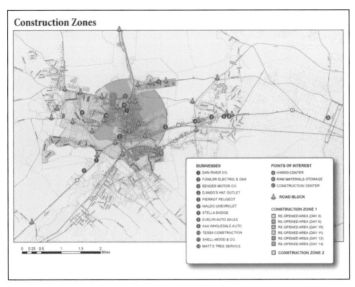

Figure 228—Inspiration Index: Maps

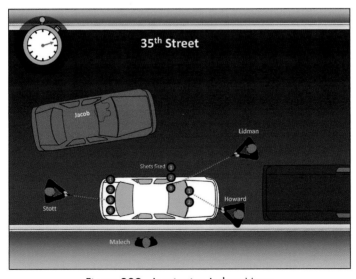

Figure 229—Inspiration Index: Maps

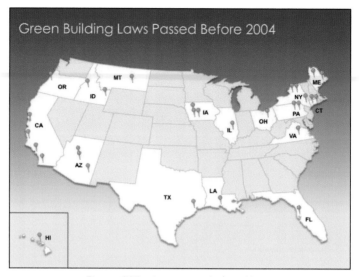

Figure 230—Inspiration Index: Maps

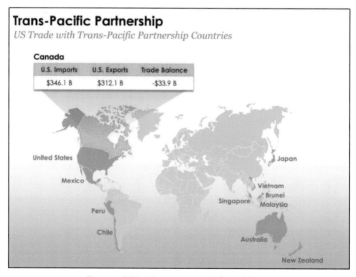

Figure 231—Inspiration Index: Maps

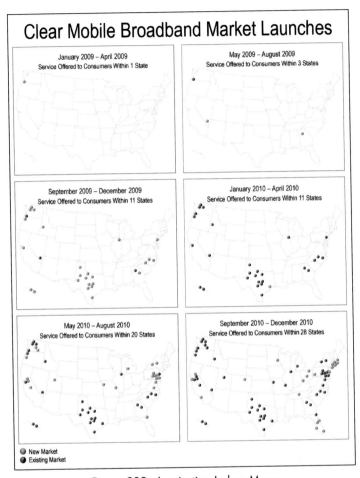

Figure 232—Inspiration Index: Maps

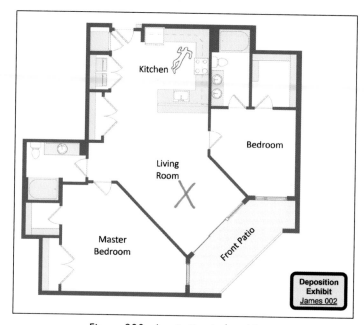

Figure 233—Inspiration Index: Maps

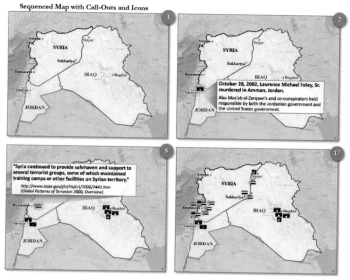

Figure 234—Inspiration Index: Maps

Organizational Charts

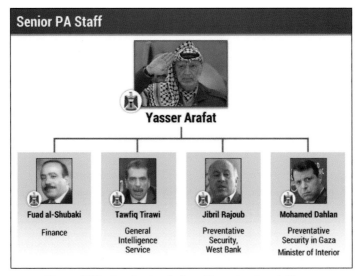

Figure 235—Inspiration Index: Organizational Charts

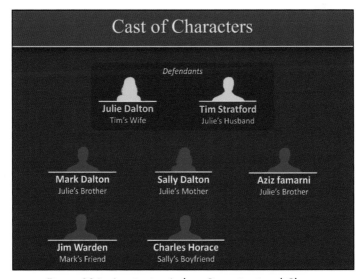

Figure 236—Inspiration Index: Organizational Charts

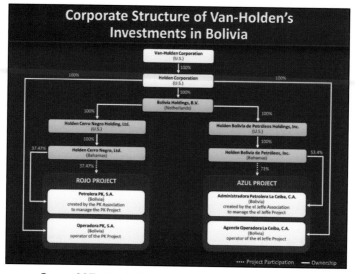

Figure 237—Inspiration Index: Organizational Charts

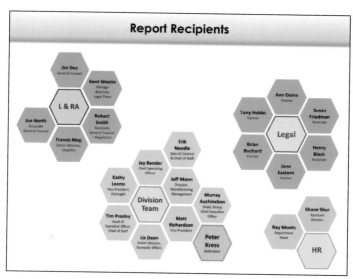

Figure 238—Inspiration Index: Organizational Charts

Figure 239—Inspiration Index: Organizational Charts

Timelines

Figure 240—Inspiration Index: Timelines

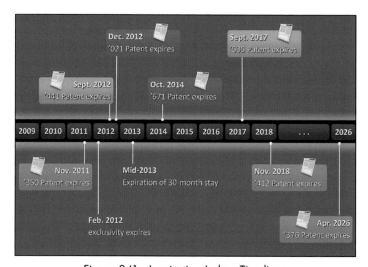

Figure 241—Inspiration Index: Timelines

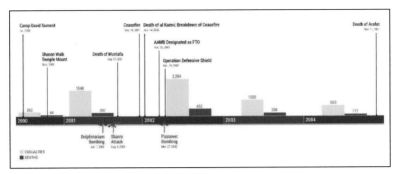

Figure 242—Inspiration Index: Timelines

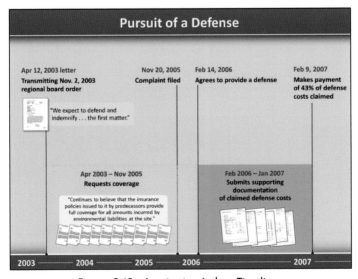

Figure 243—Inspiration Index: Timelines

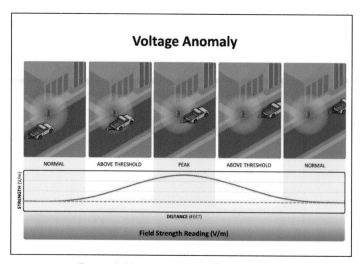

Figure 244—Inspiration Index: Timelines

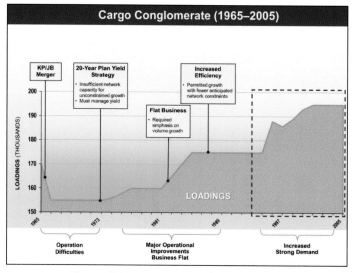

Figure 245—Inspiration Index: Timelines

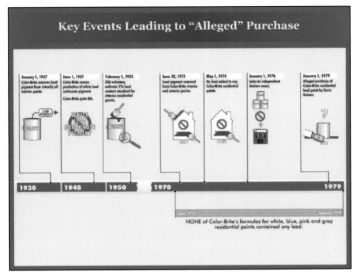

Figure 246—Inspiration Index: Timelines

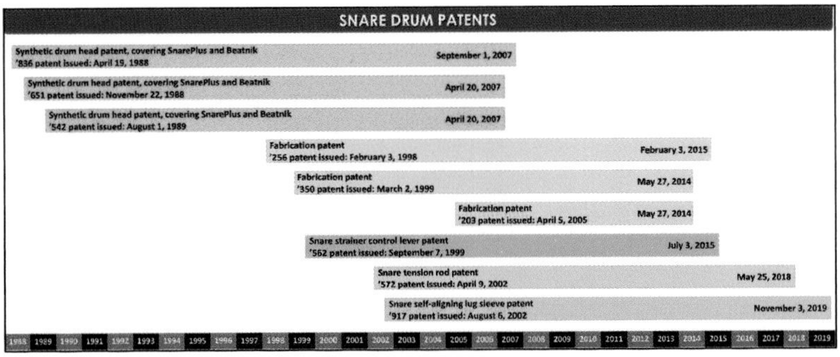

Figure 247—Inspiration Index: Timelines

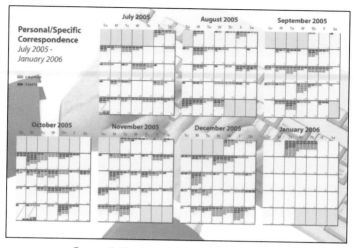

Figure 248—Inspiration Index: Timelines

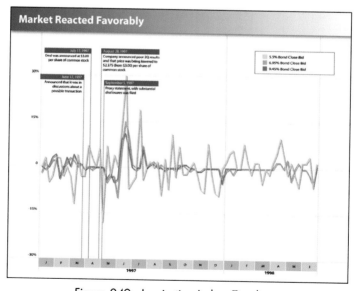

Figure 249—Inspiration Index: Timelines

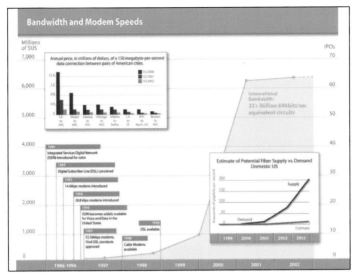

Figure 250—Inspiration Index: Timelines

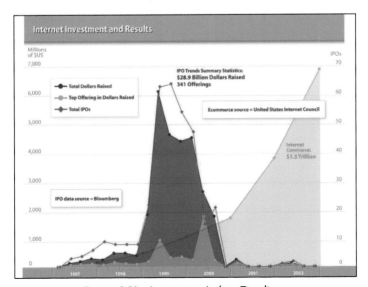

Figure 251—Inspiration Index: Timelines

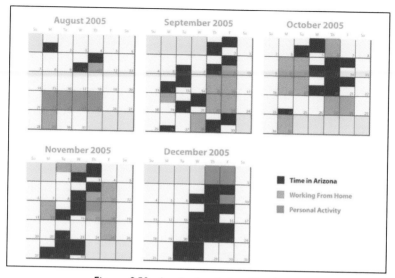

Figure 252—Inspiration Index: Timelines

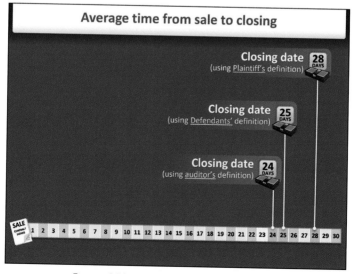

Figure 253—Inspiration Index: Timelines

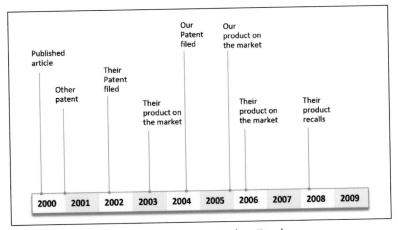

Figure 254—Inspiration Index: Timelines

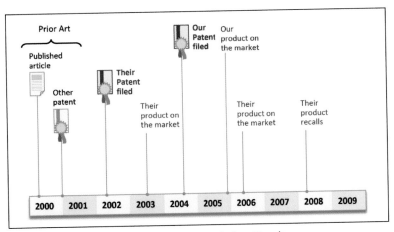

Figure 255—Inspiration Index: Timelines

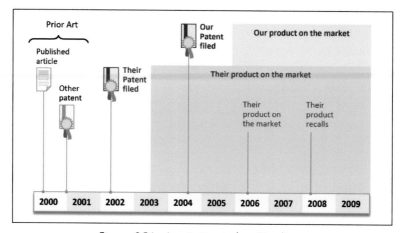

Figure 256—Inspiration Index: Timelines

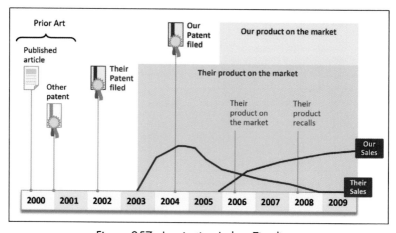

Figure 257—Inspiration Index: Timelines

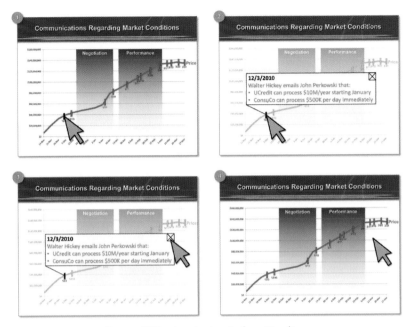

Figure 258—Inspiration Index: Timelines

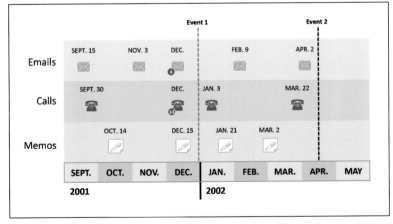

Figure 259—Inspiration Index: Timelines

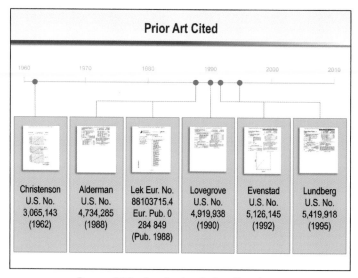

Figure 260—Inspiration Index: Timelines

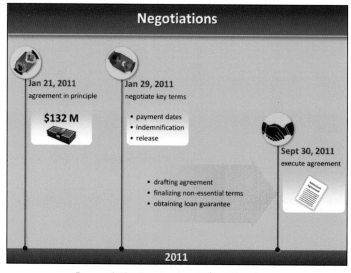

Figure 261—Inspiration Index: Timelines

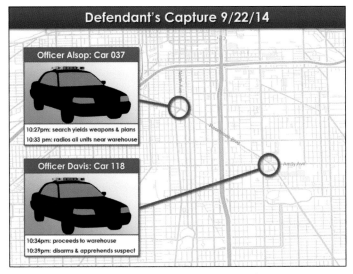

Figure 262—Inspiration Index: Timelines

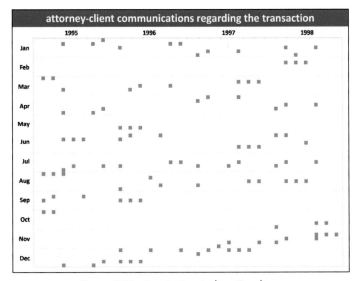

Figure 263—Inspiration Index: Timelines

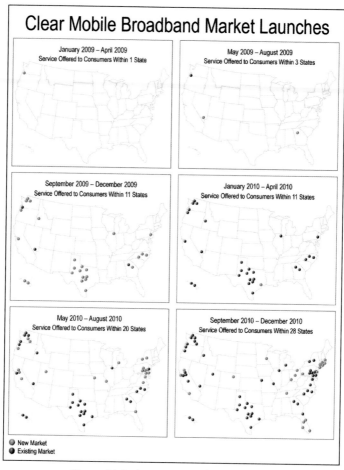

Figure 264—Inspiration Index: TImelines

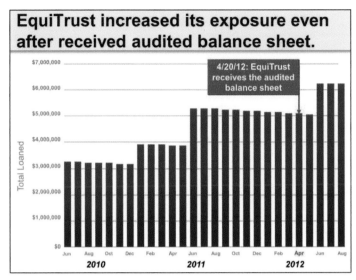

Figure 265—Inspiration Index: Timelines

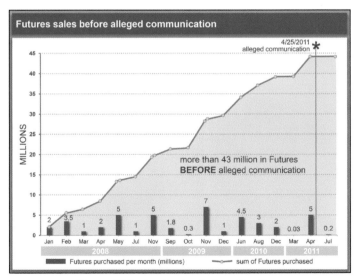

Figure 266—Inspiration Index: Timelines

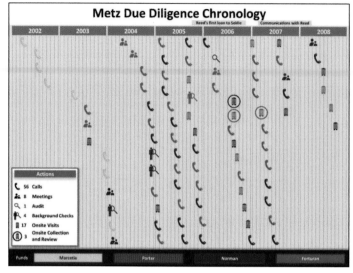

Figure 267—Inspiration Index: Timelines

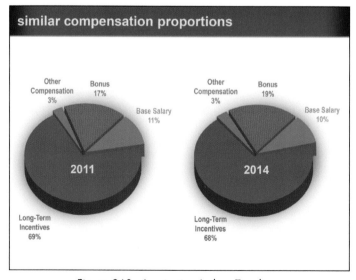

Figure 268—Inspiration Index: Timelines

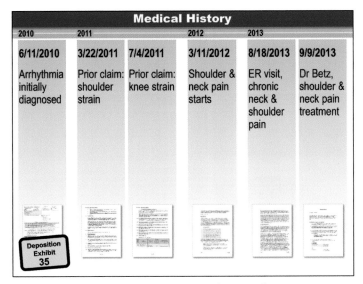

Figure 269—Inspiration Index: Timelines

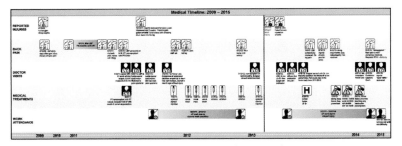

Figure 270—Inspiration Index: Timelines

2D and 3D Illustrations and Animation Stills

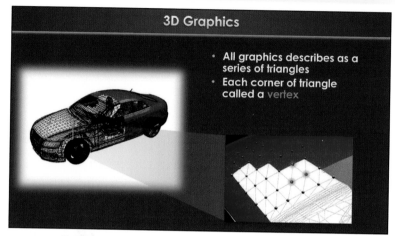

Figure 271—Inspiration Index: 2D and 3D Illustrations

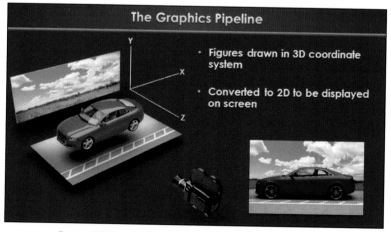

Figure 272—Inspiration Index: 2D and 3D Illustrations

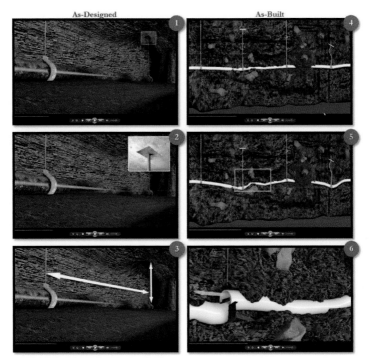

Figure 273—Inspiration Index: 2D and 3D Illustrations

Figure 274—Inspiration Index:
2D and 3D Illustrations; Animation Stills

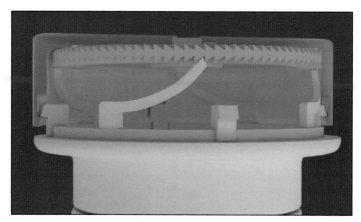

Figure 275—Inspiration Index: 2D and 3D Illustrations; Animation Stills

Figure 276—Inspiration Index: 2D and 3D Illustrations; Animation Stills

Figure 277—Inspiration Index: 2D and 3D Illustrations; Animation Stills

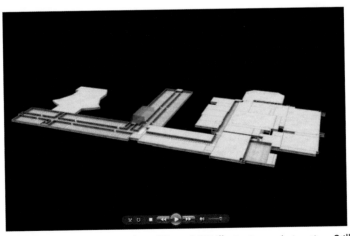

Figure 278—Inspiration Index: 2D and 3D Illustrations; Animation Stills

Figure 279—Inspiration Index: 2D and 3D Illustrations; Animation Stills

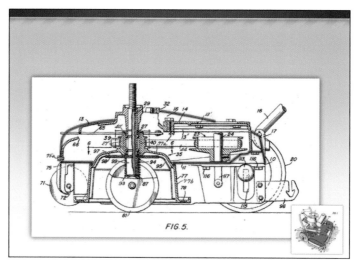

Figure 280—Inspiration Index: 2D and 3D Illustrations; Animation Stills

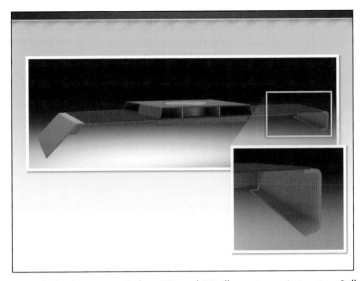

Figure 281—Inspiration Index: 2D and 3D Illustrations; Animation Stills

Figure 282—Inspiration Index: 2D and 3D Illustrations; Animation Stills

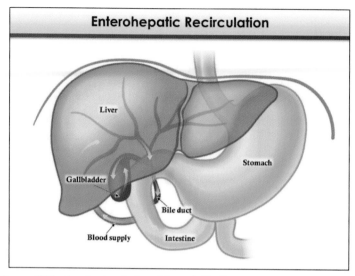

Figure 283—Inspiration Index: 2D and 3D Illustrations; Animation Stills

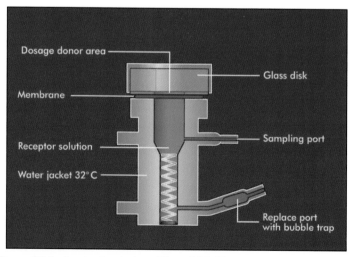

Figure 284—Inspiration Index: 2D and 3D Illustrations; Animation Stills

Figure 285—Inspiration Index: 2D and 3D Illustrations; Animation Stills

Figure 286—Inspiration Index:
2D and 3D Illustrations;
Animation Stills

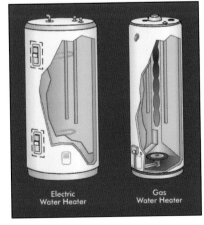

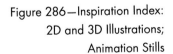

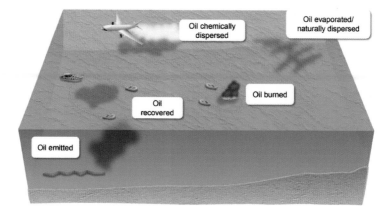

Figure 287—Inspiration Index: 2D and 3D Illustrations; Animation Stills

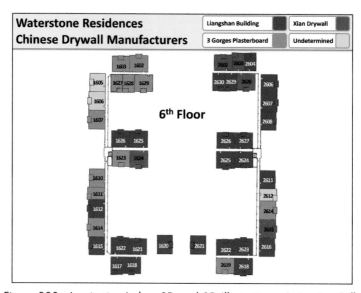

Figure 288—Inspiration Index: 2D and 3D Illustrations; Animation Stills

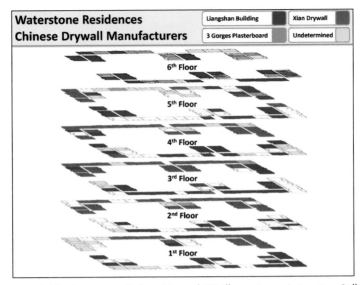

Figure 289—Inspiration Index: 2D and 3D Illustrations; Animation Stills

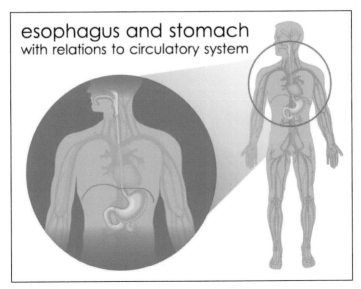

Figure 290—Inspiration Index: 2D and 3D Illustrations; Animation Stills

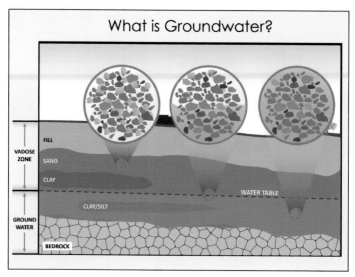

Figure 291—Inspiration Index: 2D and 3D Illustrations; Animation Stills

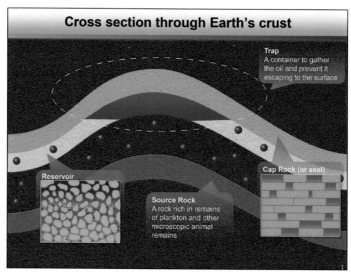

Figure 292—Inspiration Index: 2D and 3D Illustrations; Animation Stills

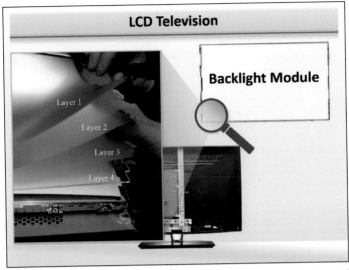

Figure 293—Inspiration Index: 2D and 3D Illustrations; Animation Stills

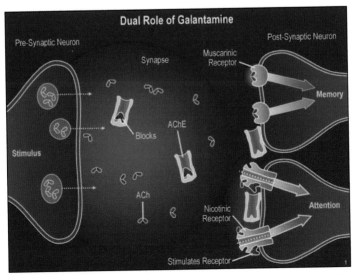

Figure 294—Inspiration Index: 2D and 3D Illustrations; Animation Stills

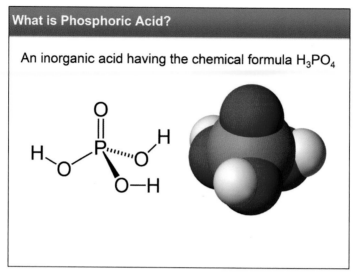

Figure 295—Inspiration Index: 2D and 3D Illustrations; Animation Stills

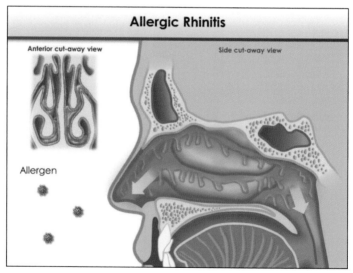

Figure 296—Inspiration Index: 2D and 3D Illustrations; Animation Stills

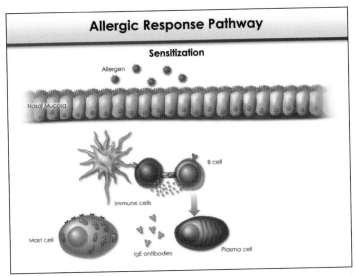

Figure 297—Inspiration Index: 2D and 3D Illustrations; Animation Stills

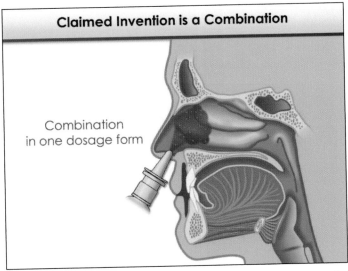

Figure 298—Inspiration Index: 2D and 3D Illustrations; Animation Stills

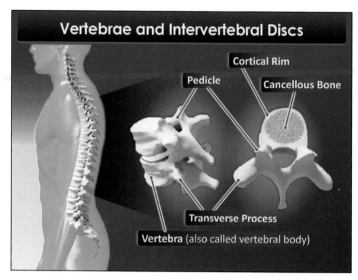

Figure 299—Inspiration Index: 2D and 3D Illustrations; Animation Stills

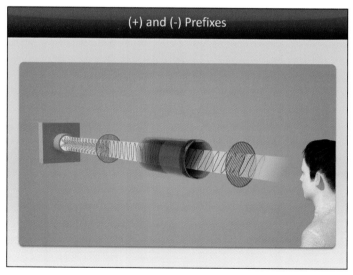

Figure 300—Inspiration Index: 2D and 3D Illustrations; Animation Stills

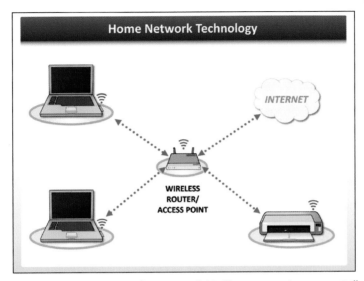

Figure 301—Inspiration Index: 2D and 3D Illustrations; Animation Stills

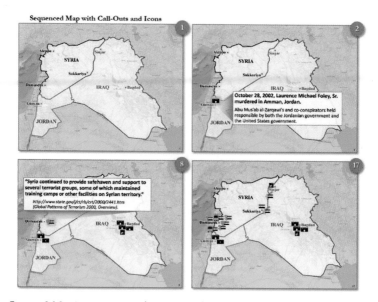

Figure 302—Inspiration Index: 2D and 3D Illustrations; Animation Stills

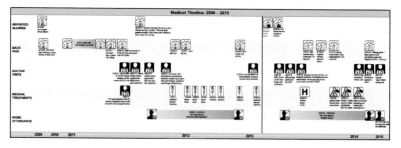

Figure 303—Inspiration Index: 2D and 3D Illustrations; Animation Stills

Figure 304—Inspiration Index: 2D and 3D Illustrations; Video Frame

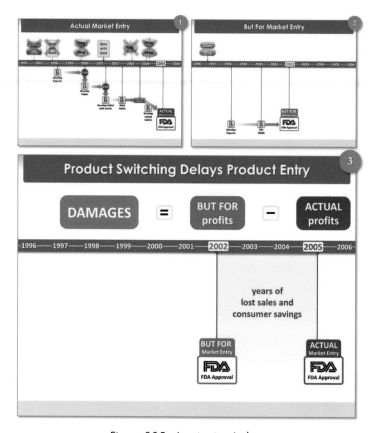

Figure 305—Inspiration Index:
2D and 3D Illustrations; Animation Stills

Figure Index

Index